STUDIES IN ECONOMIC HISTORY

This series, specially commissioned by the Economic History Society, focuses attention on the main problems of economic history. Recently there has been a great deal of detailed research and reinterpretation, some of it controversial, but it has remained largely inaccessible to students or buried in academic journals. This series is an attempt to provide a guide to the current interpretations of the key themes of economic history in which advances have recently been made, or in which there has been significant debate.

Each book will survey recent work, indicate the full scope of the particular problem as it has been opened by research and distinguish what conclusions can be drawn in the present state of knowledge. Both old and recent work will be reviewed critically, but each book will provide a balanced survey rather than an exposition of the author's own viewpoint.

The series as a whole will give readers access to the best work done, help them to draw their own conclusions in some major fields and, by means of the critical bibliography in each book, guide them in the selection of further reading. The aim is to provide a springboard to further work and not a set of pre-packaged conclusions or short cuts.

STUDIES IN ECONOMIC HISTORY

Edited for the Economic History Society by
M. W. Flinn

The Cotton Industry in the Industrial Revolution

Prepared for
The Economic History Society by

S. D. CHAPMAN

Pasold Lecturer in Textile History
in the University of Nottingham

MACMILLAN

First published 1972 by
THE MACMILLAN PRESS LTD
London and Basingstoke

Associated companies in New York Toronto
Dublin Melbourne Johannesburg and Madras

SBN 333 13584 9

Printed in Great Britain by
THE ANCHOR PRESS LTD
Tiptree, Essex

Contents

List of Tables

Acknowledgements

I SHOULD like to thank Professor A. W. Coats and Professor M. W. Flinn for their meticulous reading of the manuscript, and for important suggestions which have been included in the final version of the text. Professor L. S. Pressnell kindly directed me to the Chatham papers at the Public Record Office and so helped to illuminate an obscure aspect of the subject. I have benefited from conversations with Dr. John Butt on the Scottish cotton industry.

S. D. C.

Editor's Preface

SO long as the study of economic history was confined to only a small group at a few universities, its literature was not prolific and its few specialists had no great problem in keeping abreast of the work of their colleagues. Even in the 1930s there were only two journals devoted exclusively to this field. But the high quality of the work of the economic historians during the inter-war period and the post-war growth in the study of the social sciences sparked off an immense expansion in the study of economic history after the Second World War. There was a great expansion of research and many new journals were launched, some specialising in branches of the subject like transport, business or agricultural history. Most significantly, economic history began to be studied as an aspect of history in its own right in schools. As a consequence, the examining boards began to offer papers in economic history at all levels, while textbooks specifically designed for the school market began to be published.

For those engaged in research and writing this period of rapid expansion of economic history studies has been an exciting, if rather breathless one. For the larger numbers, however, labouring in the outfield of the schools and colleges of further education, the excitement of the explosion of research has been tempered by frustration caused by its vast quantity and, frequently, its controversial character. Nor, it must be admitted, has the ability or willingness of the academic economic historians to generalise and summarise marched in step with their enthusiasm for research.

The greatest problems of interpretation and generalisation have tended to gather round a handful of principal themes in economic history. It is, indeed, a tribute to the sound sense of economic historians that they have continued to dedicate their energies, however inconclusively, to the solution of these key problems. The results of this activity, however, much of it stored away in a wide range of academic journals, have tended to remain inaccessible to many of those currently interested in the subject. Recognising the need for guidance through the

9

burgeoning and confusing literature that has grown around these basic topics, the Economic History Society decided to launch this series of small books. The books are intended to serve as guides to current interpretations in important fields of economic history in which important advances have recently been made, or in which there has recently been some significant debate. Each book aims to survey recent work, to indicate the full scope of the particular problem as it has been opened up by recent scholarship, and to draw such conclusions as seem warranted, given the present state of knowledge and understanding. The authors will often be at pains to point out where, in their view, because of a lack of information or inadequate research, they believe it is premature to attempt to draw firm conclusions. While authors will not hesitate to review recent and older work critically, the books are not intended to serve as vehicles for their own specialist views: the aim is to provide a balanced summary rather than an exposition of the author's own viewpoint. Each book will include a descriptive bibliography.

In this way the series aims to give all those interested in economic history at a serious level access to recent scholarship in some major fields. Above all, the aim is to help the reader to draw his own conclusions, and to guide him in the selection of further reading as a means to this end, rather than to present him with a set of pre-packaged conclusions.

M. W. FLINN
Editor

University of Edinburgh

1 The Early Development of the Cotton Industry, 1600–1760

MOST of what is known about the early development of the cotton industry in Britain can be found in Wadsworth and Mann's *The Cotton Trade and Industrial Lancashire, 1600–1780*. It appears that the manufacture of cotton came to Britain from the Low Countries in the sixteenth century, one of the range of 'new draperies' that was transforming the textile industry in the later Tudor period. It was brought to East Anglia by Walloon and Dutch immigrants who settled in Norwich and other towns and established the manufacture of fustian, a mixture of linen with cotton imported from the Levant. Towards the end of the sixteenth century fustian reached Lancashire and began to oust the woollen industry from the western side of the county.

The developments that took place from this introduction to the middle of the eighteenth century cannot concern us in any detail. It is only possible to pick out the characteristics of the trade that emerged in this period and which help to explain its phenomenal success after that time. Three closely related subjects traced by Wadsworth and Mann require attention: the influence of London as a market and a supplier of raw materials and capital; the emergence of the domestic system of industrial organisation in Lancashire; and the party played by oriental influences on fashion and overseas trade generally.

Economic historians of the early modern period have rightly emphasised the important role of London in the national economy, calling on centres of regional specialisation both for the basic needs of its growing population and for the wealthy classes who were coming to regard it as proper to buy town houses and gather in the metropolis for the season. It was this growing market, fed, so far as textiles were concerned, through Blackwell Hall, that provided the major encouragement to the emergent manufacture in the seventeenth century. London dealers, often of Lancashire extraction, might employ an agent in Manchester to buy up cloth from the scattered manufacturers,

11

or Manchester fustian dealers might forward goods to Blackwell Hall, the London cloth market, on their own account. Most of the raw cotton was imported through London and forwarded to Manchester on credit terms that encouraged the northern manufacturer. By the later seventeenth century the bill of exchange drawn on London had become the predominant means of payment for Lancashire dealers, and this financial support was crucial to the development of the trade.

London also played an important role in technical innovation in the cotton industry, acting as a nursery for techniques brought from the Continent or from India until they were ready for transplanting to the provinces, where there was less competition for land, labour and capital. Thus the 'Dutch engine loom', a complicated machine that made several linen or cotton tapes at once, found its way to Manchester via London. It was introduced by alien (probably Dutch) settlers early in the seventeenth century and was in use in Manchester by the Restoration. By 1750 there were at least 1,500 Dutch looms in use in the parish of Manchester, concentrated in enlarged workshops distinct from the weavers' cottages, and Wadsworth and Mann recognise the Dutch loom workshops as a first step in the transition to the factory system.

The technique of printing fustians with bright-coloured designs was also a London industry before it migrated to the North-west to become the foundation of the Lancashire calico-printing industry. Most dyes available in the seventeenth century had a weak affinity for cotton, and the fundamental technique, copied from Indian craftsmen on the Malabar coast, was the application of mordants to fix the dye in the cloth so that it could be washed without losing its character. Calico printing was established in London by 1675 and soon began to achieve success in imitating the popular oriental designs; by 1712 'the East India Company was informing its agents that printing could be done in England at half the price charged for Indian goods and in better colours and patterns'. Unhappily this success aroused the enmity of the established woollen and silk industries, and during a prolonged agitation coinciding with the depression in trade caused by the outbreak of war with Spain in 1718, they succeeded in persuading Parliament to prohibit the sale, use and wear of English calicoes. However, the Act left two loopholes from which Lancashire was to benefit: it allowed calico printing for the export trade, and exempted the printing of fustians. In practice, English fustian was increasingly difficult to distinguish from Indian calico, and manufacturers took advantage of this similarity not only in the domestic market, but also in selling on the Continent, particularly in France, where calico printing had been banned in 1686.

The original role of Lancashire was to weave the fustian cloth which was sent to London for bleaching, printing and marketing. The fustian manufacturing process in the seventeenth and eighteenth centuries was organised on what is often called the domestic system. The entrepreneur was a merchant resident in Manchester, Bolton or Blackburn, and having trade connections with London. He distributed raw cotton and linen to a dispersed army of domestic spinners and weavers through local agents (or middlemen) called fustian manufacturers. The domestic workers were wage-earners, but they might own their own wheels and looms, and some drew support from farming activities. By the middle of the eighteenth century a large proportion of the population of Lancashire and the adjacent parts of the West Riding and Cheshire were dependent on the textile industry. Analysis of the baptismal registers shows that in the neighbourhood of Manchester from 50 to 70 per cent of the fathers recorded worked in some branch of the textile industries, while in Saddleworth (an area of some 40 square miles of gritstone Pennines between Oldham and Huddersfield) there were as many as 85 per cent.[1] The important point is that the Lancashire region saw the evolution of a capitalist class and an experienced work-force for nearly two centuries before the first water-powered cotton mills were built in the area. William Radcliffe of Mellor (near Stockport) recounted how a child brought up in a home where the cotton manufacture was carried on acquired 'a practical knowledge

[1] A. P. Wadsworth and J. de L. Mann, *The Cotton Trade and Industrial Lancashire, 1600–1780* (Manchester, 1931) esp. pp. 72–91, 314–23; M. T. Wild, 'The Saddleworth Parish Registers', *Textile History*, I (1969) p. 221.

of every process from the cotton bag to the piece of cloth', and how such training laid the foundation for an independent career in the industry during the rapid growth of the trade in the 1780s and 1790s.[2]

There was a third innovation which was nourished in London for most of the seventeenth century before migrating to the provinces. The stocking frame was invented by the Revd William Lee, an obscure Renaissance genius who came from Calverton, a village just to the north of Nottingham, and took his complex mechanism to London in the hope of obtaining royal support in 1589. He was disappointed, but his workmen settled in the capital and succeeded well enough to obtain a charter from Cromwell in 1657. Lee's frame was originally used to make silk and worsted stockings, but in 1732 a Nottingham workman succeeded in his attempts to knit cotton on the machine. By this time the East Midlands, which had retained some residual interest in the stocking frame after Lee left for London, were rapidly reasserting their right to the invention, offering cheaper labour and living costs, and freedom from the restricting ordinances of the chartered company. At the middle of the eighteenth century the merchant hosiers of Nottingham, Leicester, Derby and the satellite towns were employing large numbers of domestic framework knitters and, from small origins, were becoming a wealthy trading elite. Like the Lancashire merchants, they were still dependent on London for their market, but were becoming sufficiently independent to take the initiative in seeking both new techniques and new markets.[3]

London enterprise and capital also played the pioneer role in the early development of the factory system in the provinces. The earliest water-powered silk mill in Britain was built at Derby by Thomas Cotchett, a London silk reeler, following a lease of water rights on the Derwent in 1704. By 1707 Cotchett had installed '16 double Dutch mills', so it is possible that he was trying to apply power to the Dutch engine loom as well as

[2] W. Radcliffe, *Origins of Power Loom Weaving* (Stockport, 1828) pp. 10, 65–6.

[3] J. D. Chambers, *Nottinghamshire in the Eighteenth Century* (1932) chap. 5.

to reeling silk. Cotchett's works proved expensive and were probably not successful technically; at any rate he became bankrupt in 1713 and the mill was re-leased to Cotchett's friend John Lombe, who already had some silk-reeling machinery at work in London. Lombe and his half-brother Thomas Lombe, a wealthy London silk merchant, extended the works with the benefit of additional technical knowledge from Leghorn, where silk-reeling mills were already an important part of industrial structure. The Lombes succeeded in making the Derby silk mill pay its way, not only because John was well informed on the most up-to-date Italian technology, but also because, as manager, he succeeded in establishing a regimen of order and discipline for the 300 workers employed at the mill. The buildings and organisation at Derby were copied in six mills at Stockport between 1732 and 1768, and in others at Congleton (1754), Macclesfield (1756), Sheffield (1768) and Watford (1769), and they exercised an influence over the development of the early factory system in the cotton industry, partly because Arkwright's Derby partner, Jedediah Strutt, consciously copied the organisation of the Derby mill, and partly because the mills at Stockport and Sheffield were converted to cotton in the early and still experimental period of Arkwright's success. The history of Stockport shows that the organising ability, inventive capacity and upward social mobility that came to be regarded as characteristic of cotton were found in the town's silk industry a generation earlier.[4]

Up to this point the growth of the cotton industry has been analysed mainly from the supply side; it is now time to examine the problem of the increase in demand. Some reference has been made to the influence of oriental technique and design, and this can be examined first. Since Wadsworth and Mann completed their book, the historians of design have become keenly interested in the origins of printed textiles and their expertise has radically improved our understanding of the subject. In their *Origins of Chintz*, John Irwin and Katharine Brett show that the East India Company at first imported

[4] W. H. Chaloner, *People and Industries* (1963) chap. 1; G. Unwin et al., *Samuel Oldknow and the Arkwrights* (Manchester, 1924) pp. 23–9.

15

Indian fabrics only as novelties or curiosities, mainly using them as exchange in the spice trade with Malaya. However, by 1643 the Company's directors were beginning to realise the possibilities of the home market, and instructed their agents that the design of imported chintzes should respond to taste in the London market. By 1669 the directors were sending out patterns to be copied, and ordering 2,000 pieces at a time. To keep pace with the accelerating demand, English and Dutch traders settled Indian cotton painters within the protected area of their own trading stations. British governments' attempts to restrict the calico trade in 1700 and 1720 never achieved total prohibition, and the competition of the East India Company's factories continued to present a challenge to English manufacturers to improve their craftsmanship until the end of the eighteenth century.[5]

Some reference has already been made to the large export of printed cottons at the middle of the eighteenth century. For the first three-quarters of the century, until the new technology began to undermine the competitive position of Continental producers, most of the overseas demand came from Africa (where brightly printed cottons were exchanged for cargoes of slaves for the West Indian or Virginian plantations) and from the American and West Indian colonists. As Wadsworth and Mann explain, this highly successful trade 'was prophetic of Lancashire's later pre-eminence in providing for warm climates and coloured races'. It was the carefully cultivated domestic and overseas market, rather than superior technology, that was the key to British achievement in the cotton industry until after the middle of the eighteenth century.

[5] J. Irwin and K. Brett, *Origins of Chintz* (1970) pp. 3–6. See also F. M. Montgomery, *Printed Textiles: English and American Cottons and Linens, 1700–1850* (1970).

2 Technology

THE technical developments that laid the foundation of the nineteenth-century success of the cotton industry have received more attention than any other aspect of its history. The literature on Hargreaves's jenny, Arkwright's water frame, Crompton's mule, and the ancillary preparation machinery, is so abundant that a new description, even of the salient features, seems unnecessary, and in any case students of economic history are more interested in the significance of innovations than in the details of inventions. This section will therefore be confined to three features of technical change in the cotton industry which are essential to an appreciation of the process of economic growth: the adoption of mechanical power, the increase in productivity, and the stages in the transition from the domestic to the factory system.

The distinction between the factory system and the workshop system of production cannot be defined exclusively in terms of the use of mechanical power; it also requires concentration of the processes of manufacture under one roof, the use of specialised machines, and the organisation and direction of the labour force by specialised management. Nevertheless, the availability of power is the physical prerequisite of success, and therefore forms a suitable starting-point for this survey. The traditional forms of power were the horse gin (i.e. a horse harnessed to a capstan), windmills and water mills, and all three were in use in the cotton industry in the period covered by this book, though so far as is known windmills were only used to return water to reservoirs and so augment the supply to water wheels.

Richard Arkwright and his partners found their roller spinning machine too heavy for manual operation and so had to install a horse capstan in their first factory (a converted house in Nottingham) in 1769, and many of those who copied the technique at first used the same source of power. Horse capstans were cheap to install (insurance records show that they were seldom valued at more than £50) and particularly suited to the stage at which small fustian manufacturers or hosiers were adapting existing premises to factory production, either for warp spinning (Arkwright's technique) or, a little later, for the carding engine and power-assisted mule. Horse capstans were indeed so common that few contemporaries thought them worthy of note, but scattered references suggest that they were possibly the most common kind of power installation until the end of the century, and formed an important stepping-stone from domestic to factory production.[6]

However this may be, there can be little doubt that water wheels provided most of the power for the cotton industry until after 1820. Early in the eighteenth century the traditional paddle (or 'undershot') water wheels began to be replaced by the more efficient breast and overshot wheels, particularly after John Smeaton, the most famous engineer of the age, demonstrated the increased power of the latter with experimental models in some lectures to the Royal Society in London in 1751.[7] The power requirements of the cotton industry were at first quite modest (it has been estimated that in 1795 the whole of the year's import of cotton could have been spun with 5,000 h.p.) and, in the Pennines, where a typical minor stream draining into the Manchester embayment could generate more than 400 h.p., increased power demands appear to have been met without an immediate shortage of water power. Again, the importance of this factor is that costs were kept low during the crucial pioneer years, enabling entrepreneurs of limited resources to enter or retain a place in the industry.

By the middle of the eighteenth century the Newcomen steam engine was employed in most mining districts for drainage, and was soon at work replenishing reservoirs in locations of the textile industry where coal was plentiful and cheap. Local shortages of water power, especially on the Midland plain and the urban centres of the cotton industry, compelled factory owners who wanted to remain on the same site to consider the possibility of using James Watt's rotary steam engine in direct

[6] R. L. Hills, *Power in the Industrial Revolution* (Manchester, 1970) pp. 66–7; J. Tann, *The Development of the Factory* (1970) pp. 47–9.

[7] D. S. L. Cardwell, 'Power Technologies and the Advance of Science, 1700–1825', *Technology and Culture*, VI (1965).

transmission to carding and spinning machinery. Several of the leaders of the industry, notably Arkwright, the Peels and Major Cartwright (brother of the inventor Edmund Cartwright), were involved in some costly failures with pioneer steam mills, and those who persevered complained of high maintenance costs, slow after-sales service and, above all, capital and running costs much in excess of a water wheel on a good stream. The cost of power is very difficult to calculate for this period as data are scarce, and every water-power site involved the buyer or lessee in a different outlay and presented its own individual return to the investment; but such evidence as is available points to the conclusion that those occupying sites yielding more than 10 to 20 h.p. found them competitive until the late 1830s, when the optimum scale of factory production began to increase.[8]

Unfortunately, there are no general surveys of the comparative importance of water and steam power until 1835, when the steam engine, after more than half a century of continuous improvement, had become the predominant form of power in every cotton town in the North of England except a few Pennine centres like Glossop, Mottram and Halifax. By that time, as the figures[9] in Table 1 show, steam was responsible for three-quarters of the power used in the industry. The table draws

TABLE 1

WATER AND STEAM POWER IN 1835

	No. of mills	Steam h.p.	Water h.p.
Northern region	934	26,513	6,094
Scotland	125	3,200	2,480
Midlands	54	438	c. 1,200
Total	1,113	30,151	c. 9,774

particular attention to the dominance of the Northern region (i.e. Lancashire and the adjacent parts of Cheshire, Derbyshire

[8] S. D. Chapman, 'The Cost of Power in the Industrial Revolution', *Midland History*, I (1971).

[9] Extracted from E. Baines, *History of the Cotton Manufacture* (1835) pp. 386–92.

19

and the West Riding), which was clearly secured by steam power. At the end of the eighteenth century this region had contributed something like 70 per cent of the cotton manufacture; but in 1835 it had reached 90 per cent. Steam power was still as expensive as water power, but its use was economised, partly by specialisation on manually operated power-*assisted* mules, partly by the increasing concentration of the cotton industry on the Lancashire coalfield. In the peripheral areas the older roller spinning technique of Arkwright, extravagant with the more abundant water-power resources of the Peak district and Scotland, continued to specialise on coarse spinning.[10] However, these distinctions demand some basic appreciation of the nature of the two principal methods of production, and warrant closer examination.

The most important features of the introduction of mechanised carding and spinning are the spectacular increase in output, the fundamental improvement in quality of yarns, and the continuous trend of falling prices. The easiest way of illustrating the quantitive change is to reproduce the data on labour productivity in Catling's study of *The Spinning Mule*, where the modern concept of O.H.P. (i.e. the number of Operative Hours to Process 100 lb. of cotton) is applied to historical situations (see Table 2). The only qualification that

TABLE 2

LABOUR PRODUCTIVITY IN COTTON SPINNING

Indian hand spinners (18th cent.)	50,000 + O.H.P.	
Crompton's mule (1780)	2,000	,,
100-spindle mule (*c.* 1790)	1,000	,,
Power-assisted mules (*c.* 1795)	300	,,
Roberts's automatic mules (*c.* 1825)	135	,,
Most efficient machinery today (1972)	40	,,

must be made to this table is that there was frequently a time-lag between the introduction of improved machinery and its widespread adoption. Catling's estimates do not cover the

[10] H. B. Rodgers, 'The Lancashire Cotton Industry in 1840', *Transactions of the Institute of British Geographers*, xxviii (1960).

older (Arkwright) technique of roller spinning, but it is possible to make calculations from contemporary descriptions of mills.[11] Specifications of the most efficient mills suggest that they fell within the 250–370 O.H.P. range in the 1780s and 1790s, i.e. that productivity was as high as in mule spinning during the pioneer years.[12] The labour force at Arkwright-type mills was mostly unskilled females and juveniles on low wages, while mules were operated by men whose skill was scarce and expensive, so that as long as the two systems could compete in quality, entrepreneurs with capital pursued the Arkwright system.

The quality of yarn was the decisive factor in the competition between the rival systems. The traditional one-thread hand wheel spun 'little or no thread finer than 16 to 20 hanks in the pound, each hank measuring 840 yards', and evenness depended on the delicacy of touch of the spinner. (This degree of fineness – the count of the yarn – was expressed, by trade convention, as 16s to 20s, and other achievements *pro rata*.) Hargreaves's jenny, duplicating the motions of the hand spinner, reached the low 20s, while Arkwright, at the pinnacle of his achievement, attained 60s.[13] Apart from calico printing, the competition was principally focused on quantity rather than quality up to this time. The manufacture of fine articles still depended on highly skilled workers, and the Swiss towns of Zürich, Wädenswil, Horgen, Stäfa and St Gall had practically the European monopoly; the only competition attempted was from the cambric manufacturers at St Quentin and Tarare, towards 1756, and Glasgow in 1769. Crompton's mule, which was soon spinning 80s, and reached 300s by the end of the century, transformed the situation almost overnight. Thomas Ainsworth at Bolton (1780) and Samuel Oldknow at Anderton and Stockport (1782–4) began making muslins, and three years later, in 1787, Britain already produced 500,000 pieces.

[11] H. Catling, *The Spinning Mule* (Newton Abbot, 1970) p. 54.

[12] Calculations based on data in Portland MSS., Notts. C.R.O., DD 4P 79/63, and Chatham papers, P.R.O., 30/8/187.

[13] Abraham Rees, *Cyclopaedia*, article on 'Cotton' (1808); C. Aspin, *James Hargreaves and the Spinning Jenny* (Helmshore, Lancs., 1964).

The number of mule spindles increased from something like 50,000 in 1788 to 4·6 million in 1811.[14]

Textbook accounts of industrialisation in Britain and on the Continent have often drawn a distinction between 'mass-produced' British goods and the products of the more fashion- and design-conscious French. In cotton textiles the distinction cannot be sustained after 1790. The branches of the trade most sensitive to fashion were calico printing and lace, and in both the British had demonstrated their superiority in the third quarter of the eighteenth century. In calico printing, the advances in dyeing and printing technique mentioned in the last section were now reinforced by improvements in spinning and by the rapid adoption of the chemical bleaching technique discovered by Berthollet in France in 1785.

Lancashire success in the mechanisation of fine spinning not only absorbed the enterprise and capital of the region in the 1780s and 1790s, but also began to divert capital from Arkwright's system. By 1795, when M'Connel & Kennedy of Manchester succeeded in applying a Boulton & Watt steam engine to the two 'heavy' motions of the four-movement cycle of the mule, many of the pioneers of the Arkwright system, like the Peels and Douglases, began to direct their investment into the new and rapidly developing technique, though the older system (as Strutt's experience illustrates) continued to provide prosperity for a number of efficient firms. Consequently, mule spinning quickly superseded warp spinning in importance, and was the predominant system for the remainder of the period covered by this study. The only exception to this generalisation was the early 1830s, when investment in power looms, which were at first only suitable for the coarser yarns, led to a temporary revival of interest in warp spinning.[15]

[14] M. Lévy-Leboyer, *Les Banques Européennes et l'Industrialisation Internationale* (Paris, 1964) p. 27.

[15] S. D. Chapman, 'Fixed Capital Formation in the British Cotton Manufacturing Industry', in J. P. P. Higgins and S. Pollard (eds.), *Aspects of Capital Investment in Great Britain, 1750–1850* (1971) pp. 72–3; R. S. Fitton and A. P. Wadsworth, *The Strutts and the Arkwrights* (Manchester, 1958) pp. 196–8.

Spinning by power commands more attention than an other technique because it set in motion a sequence of technical and organisational changes in connected branches of the industry. Success at the spinning stage of the production process immediately created the need for an increase of output at the earlier stages, and all the important inventors of spinning machines were compelled to divert their minds to preparation machinery. The cotton from the bale had to be picked and cleaned, 'batted' (or beaten, to open the fibres), carded into a continuous sliver, 'drawn' (to lay the fibres parallel) and 'roved' (to attenuate the sliver) before it reached the spinning frames, and in the lifetime of Arkwright and Crompton a community of fertile minds in the Lancashire cotton towns succeeded in mechanising these processes. The outcome was the perfection of a system of continuous (or flow) production in which the cotton was mechanically handled from the moment the bales were hoisted from the drays to the top floor of the mill to that at which it was dispatched, in carefully graded yarns, from the ground-floor warehouse. Rapid dispersion of these ideas was the work of a corps of specialised millwrights and machine builders, who erected the mill buildings and machinery on uniform lines, originally imitating the achievements of Arkwright, Peel and other pioneers.[16]

The Hargreaves and Arkwright techniques of spinning superseded the old hand spinning wheels with a speed that, in retrospect, appeared almost dramatic. In 1768-9 there were some angry demonstrations in the Blackburn area by people who feared unemployment, but the general experience was probably reflected by William Radcliffe's comment on the change at Mellor (Stockport). 'The hands, turned adrift from hand cards and the spinning wheel, soon found full employ in the loom on machine yarn, with three to four fold more wages than they had been able to earn in their own trade . . .', he recalled. Some families with no reserves of capital, Radcliffe infers, were forced out of the industry, but for those with initiative there was a golden opportunity to earn unprecedented

[16] Hills, *Power in the Industrial Revolution*, chap. v; Chapman, 'Fixed Capital Formation', pp. 61-3.

wages and establish themselves as independent manufacturers.[17]

The rising costs that led to the era of inventions in the spinning section of the industry found a parallel in some other sections, particularly weaving, knitting, bleaching, dyeing and calico printing. Wadsworth and Mann wrote of a 'rapid transition to industrial capitalism' in these later stages of production between 1750 and 1780, and though they were evidently reviewing a variety of precocious enterprises rather than the typical firm, there can be no doubt that the period saw considerable growth in the size of workshops. Weaving looms and knitting frames were beginning to be concentrated in workshops employing supervised wage-earners, either to reduce the time wasted in distributing raw materials and collecting goods from domestic workers, or to improve the quality of the finished product. By the early nineteenth century, according to Bythell, there were isolated weaving sheds 'with as many as 150 or 200 handlooms, quite a few with between 50 and 100, and a considerable number with 20 or more. Such sheds were to be found in town and country throughout the weaving area.' This development, Bythell maintains, 'represented a half-way stage between true domestic industry and the modern power-driven weaving shed'. There is no comparable information on numbers employed in bleaching, but in Scotland the bleach yards for linen, which used the same techniques and were often converted to cotton, are said to have commonly employed 80 to 100 workers before the end of the eighteenth century. In the printing section of the industry there is also evidence of concentrations of labour and capital. The leviathan of the industry, Livesey, Hargreaves & Co. of Blackburn, employed between 700 and 1,000 printers shortly before their bankruptcy in 1788.[18]

The traditional bleaching technique involved repeated immersions of the cloth in sour milk (lactic acid), followed by weeks of tentering in the open fields to allow the sun to complete

[17] Wadsworth and Mann, *The Cotton Trade*, pp. 477–80; Radcliffe, *Origins of Power Loom Weaving*, p. 62.

[18] D. Bythell, *The Handloom Weavers* (Cambridge, 1969) p. 33; Wadsworth and Mann, *The Cotton Trade*, p. 307; E. Gauldie, 'Mechanical Aids to Linen Bleaching in Scotland', *Textile History*, I (1969) p. 129.

the process. The whole process lasted seven or eight months in all. Dr John Roebuck's sulphuric acid plants in Birmingham (1746) and Prestonpans, Scotland (1749), inaugurated a sharp decline in the price of this industrial chemical, and it was soon replacing sour milk in bleaching, reducing the process to about four months. However, the most drastic economy of time, as a result of which bleaching lasted little more than a day, was not made until the end of the century. Charles Tennant of Glasgow, exploiting the discoveries of Berthollet, Scheele, and pioneer plants in Manchester, Nottingham, Aberdeen and other centres of the cotton industry, successfully launched the commercial manufacture of bleaching powder. The new techniques called for specialised knowledge of chemistry, and bleaching powder manufacturers seldom had interests in spinning or weaving,[19] though a few of them were also active as dyers and printers. Both bleachworks and dyeworks used water wheels through the period covered by this study, the former to power 'wash wheels' and 'dash wheels' (hammers to wash and pound the cloth free of acid), the latter to grind down dyewoods. Mechanical power was introduced to calico printing from about 1785, when Livesey, Hargreaves & Co. began to install copper cylinders at their printworks.

Weaving and knitting were technically more difficult to subject to the water wheel and steam engine, and when efficient machines were finally developed (in weaving in the 1830s, in knitting in the 1850s), their adoption was inhibited by the poor wages of handloom weavers and framework knitters. The earliest patents for a power loom were taken out by the Revd Edmund Cartwright in 1786–8, and he and his brother (Major John Cartwright) tried to develop the invention in factories at Doncaster and Retford (Notts.), but neither succeeded. Cartwright's loom was brought to commercial success by Radcliffe, Horrocks, Marsland and other Stockport manufacturers in the first years of the nineteenth century, but the general adoption of their looms was deferred until the investment booms of 1823–5 and 1832–4. In 1833 there were esti-

[19] A. E. Musson and E. Robinson, *Science and Technology in the Industrial Revolution* (Manchester, 1969) chap. 8.

mated to be 100,000 power looms in Britain, a number which can be compared with 250,000 handloom weavers.[20] Meanwhile a major new advance was taking place in mechanised spinning, and it was this and the power looms that dictated a multiplication of the scale of the most efficient factories.

The change in scale began in the middle 1830s with the widespread adoption of Roberts's automatic mule. In 1832 an expert wrote that 'self-acting mules have long been a desideratum in the trade and have occupied the attention of intelligent managers and mechanics for some years past; [but] although several have been invented and secured by patent yet none seem to be possessed of sufficient merit to cause any excitement in the trade; in fact they seem so unimportant as to be seldom spoken of . . .' Eight years later he was producing detailed calculations to show that automatic mules were 15 per cent cheaper to operate than hand mules. Meanwhile, Dr Andrew Ure was publicising a new type of mill designed specifically for automatic mules by William Fairbairn, who was reaching the peak of his career as a Manchester millwright.[21] In 1822 the representative size of the Manchester cotton mill was still 100 to 200 hands, and in the satellite towns it was probably even smaller. This impression was confirmed in another technical work, where a representative factory unit whose costs were 'all calculated from the cost and expense of establishments that have been lately erected' was only a little larger than the Arkwright prototype, though it contained 4,500 spindles and 128 power looms and cost just over £8,000. The new mills, by contrast, contained 40,000 spindles and cost over £80,000 – an increase of ten times the capacity of the familiar scale of production. For over fifty years mules had been operated by highly skilled and semi-independent artisans on standard piece-rates, and there was no particular economy in concentration of their numbers; experience showed that the optimum production was

[20] Baines, *History of the Cotton Manufacture*, pp. 228–40.

[21] James Montgomery, *Carding and Spinning Master's Assistant* (Glasgow, 1832) p. 170, and *A Practical Detail of the Cotton Manufacture of the U.S.A. . . . compared with that of Great Britain* (Glasgow, 1840) pp. 75–81; A. Ure, *The Cotton Manufacture of Great Britain* (1836) pp. 297–313.

reached with 264–288 spindles. But the perfection of Roberts's work enabled one man, with the help of two or three boys, to work 1,600 spindles as easily as he had previously worked 300, and mills were doubled in width to accommodate the much enlarged machines.[22] These details may try the patience of those who lack interest in technical problems, but a basic appreciation of the scale and timing of technical change is essential for adequate understanding of such problems as the structure of enterprise and of industry, of capital formation and of labour relations, that follow.

[22] Chapman, 'Fixed Capital Formation', pp. 76–81.

3 The Structure of Industry and Capital Requirements

ALL the early estimates of the number and size of cotton mills in Britain are based on an estimate of the number of Arkwright-type factories and a calculation of the supposed value of these investments (see Tables 3 and 4). Colquhoun's mill census in 1787 seems fairly accurate, but he thought the mills were all of 2,000 spindles and cost £5,000 each to build, while in fact most were built on the model of Arkwright's smaller (1,000 spindle) mills. Consequently, his estimates of £715,000 (1787) and £775,000 (1790) for fixed capital are too high, and £500,000 would be nearer the true figure. Colquhoun made no estimate of capital invested in weaving, dyeing, bleaching and printing, and indeed no one else did so before 1834.

The next two estimates summarised in Table 3 were synthesised from insurance policies taken out for cotton mills. Critics of this technique complain that most property was under-insured at the period, and in general this appears to be true; but the peculiar vulnerability of cotton mills to fire risk, and the considerable losses sustained by the Sun, Royal Exchange, Phoenix and other companies in the early 1790s, ensured that such hazardous risks were subjected to the closest scrutiny by insurer and insured. The author's estimate for 1795 fixed capital is largely based on data extracted from fire insurance registers of the period, but falls back on estimates of £5,000 for the larger and £3,000 for the smaller Arkwright-type mills when insurance policies have not survived for known mills. Policies extant for a large number of mills show that these were typical figures for buildings and plant (including the power unit) at this period. The much more heterogeneous mule factories proved difficult to locate, and the figure given for these numerous small concerns is inevitably less reliable. The 1797 estimate, which is published here for the first time, was made by Hugh Watts, Secretary of the Sun Fire Office from 1786 to 1806. He had access to some 900 current policies for cotton mills, but unfortunately was too ignorant of technology to distinguish between Arkwright-type mills and mule factories.

However, taken in conjunction with the author's estimate, it appears that the 900 factories in 1797 consisted of about 300 Arkwright mills, and twice as many on Crompton's principles, though at this period the latter were generally much smaller and often housed in converted premises, a fact which is implicitly acknowledged in Watts's downward adjustment of his final estimate. In 1795 there were at least fifty of these small mule-spinning firms in Stockport alone, usually renting converted houses or factory space, where they insured machinery for from £50 to £2,000. Only two or three of the largest of them had as much insured capital as the smallest owners of water-powered factories in and about the town.

The number of firms in the industry was significantly less than the number of factories, for several leading firms had two or more factories. Peels, the biggest firm in 1795, had twenty-three mills centred on Blackburn, Bury, Bolton, Burton upon Trent and Tamworth; William Douglas and his partners had nine, divided between Pendleton (Manchester), Holywell (North Wales coast), Carlisle and Scotland; and Robinsons of Nottingham, who are regularly mentioned in the textbooks as the first firm to buy a Watt steam engine for a cotton mill, had five mills strung along a stream just to the north of the town. David Dale, lately Arkwright's partner in Scotland, had two large mills with two others being built. The great majority of entrepreneurs in the industry were, however, men of much more limited means, dragging themselves up the economic ladder by their bootstraps.[23]

Although the stresses of the French Wars persuaded some moneyed entrepreneurs to withdraw from the industry, and weeded out many of the struggling small men, the structure of the industry continued to be polarised, that is, characterised by a few giants and many small men dependent on the credit of merchants or merchant-manufacturers. By 1812, when the next survey of the industry was taken, mule spinning had easily overtaken roller spinning in importance, but this did not terminate the business careers of all the old leaders. When M'Connel & Kennedy showed the successful application of

[23] Chapman, 'Fixed Capital Formation'.

TABLE 3

ESTIMATES OF THE NUMBER OF AND FIXED CAPITAL INVESTED IN BRITISH COTTON-SPINNING MILLS, 1787–1812

Estimate	Date	Number of Arkwright-type factories	Number of mule factories and workshops	Value of an Arkwright mill	Adjustment for mule factories	Total fixed capital (£m.)	Revised total (£m.)
Colquhoun	1787	143	n.d.	£5,000	+£285,000	1·0	0·5
Chapman	1795	c. 300	n.d.	£3–5,000	+£500,000	2·0	2·0
Watts	1797	——900——		£3,000	−£200,000	2·7	2·5
Crompton	1812	n.d.	673	n.d.	(none)	3·0–4·0	5·0–6·0

Sources: P. Colquhoun, *An Important Crisis in the Calico and Muslin Manufactory . . . Explained* (1788) p.4; S. D. Chapman, 'Fixed Capital Formation in the British Cotton Industry, 1770–1815', *Economic History Review*, 2nd ser., XXIII (1970); Chatham papers, P.R.O., 30/8/187; G. W. Daniels, 'Samuel Crompton's Census of the Cotton Industry in 1811', *Economic History*, II (1930–3), and comments by Chapman, loc. cit.

Table 4

ESTIMATES OF FIXED AND WORKING CAPITAL IN THE BRITISH COTTON INDUSTRY, 1834–56

		Spinning and weaving				
		Fixed Capital	Working capital	Total	Finishing trades	Total capital
Estimate	Date	(£m.)	(£m.)	(£m.)	(£m.)	(£m.)
McCulloch	1834	14·8	7·4	22·2	11·8	34·0
Baynes	1856	31·0	14·5	45·5	30·0	75·5

Source: Estimates collected and revised by M. Blaug, 'The Productivity of Capital in the Lancashire Cotton Industry during the Nineteenth Century', *Economic History Review*, 2nd ser., XIII (1961).

Watt's steam engine to the 'heavy' motions of the mule, the giants of the industry began to switch their capital to the new system. In 1812, 70 per cent (or 472 out of 673) of the firms in mule spinning had fewer than 10,000 spindles, but a few firms had many times this number: Samuel Horrocks of Preston had 107,000 in eight mills, while Peter Marsland of Stockport, M'Connel & Kennedy, and A. & G. Murray of Manchester, each had over 80,000, to mention only the leaders. The first two were second-generation firms that had pioneered the industry, the second two machine builders who had begun in the early 1790s with very little capital.[24] The leaders of 1795 had disappeared from the top of the table, but this is partly explained by the limitations of the 1812 census, which did not count Arkwright-type mills unless they were also used for mule spinning, and extended to only sixty miles around Manchester. Big firms like the Strutts, Arkwrights, Oldknow and Peels at Tamworth and Burton upon Trent, and Douglases at Holywell, were thus excluded by definition. Evidence to a Parliamentary Committee in 1815–16 adds some details on the size of the work-force in some of the best-known concerns. Robert Owen, the successor to David Dale at New Lanark, was employing 1,600–1,700, James Finlay & Co. 1,529 at three mills in Scotland, the Strutts 1,494 at Belper (near Derby), A. & G. Murray 1,215, and M'Connel & Kennedy 1,020.[25] Nevertheless, small entrepreneurs continued to make their way into the industry, especially in the early 1820s.[26]

During the thirty-five years from the close of the Napoleonic Wars to the end of the period covered by this study, estimates suggest that fixed capital invested in the industry increased rapidly, perhaps trebling in the first two decades of peace, and doubling in the next twenty years (see Tables 3 and 4). Much of this capital was employed in enlarging and rebuilding the

[24] G. W. Daniels, 'Samuel Crompton's Census of the Cotton Industry in 1811', *Economic History*, II (1930–3) pp. 107–10.

[25] J. H. Clapham, 'Some Factory Statistics of 1815–16', *Economic Journal*, xxv (1915).

[26] E. Butterworth, *Historical Sketches of Oldham* (1856) pp. 140, 153, 183, shows that from 1821 to 1825 the number of Oldham cotton manufacturers rose from 60 to 139.

existing factories to reach optimum size rather than in multiplying their numbers, to judge from the fact that the 900 'factories' of 1797 had barely reached 1,200 in 1834, while the raw material consumed rose from 30 million to 300 million lb. It has sometimes been argued that the inventions of the Industrial Revolution had a capital-saving effect because they reduced the large working capital that was needed to span the long period between purchase of raw materials and receipt of payments for finished goods. The accounts of cotton firms of the period always show that working capital was much bigger than fixed capital, so that a reduction in the time required for production and sale could have liberated working capital for investment in buildings, machinery and land. The plausibility of this theory depends on other variables remaining constant, and there are signs that the period of credit allowed by merchant-manufacturers lengthened in the 1790s, a development which might have absorbed the capital released. However, if the theory can be accepted, it helps to explain how small manufacturers managed to sustain such a phenomenal rate of growth in the period 1797–1834.

Between 1838, when the returns allow detailed geographical analysis for the first time, and the middle of the century, the small uneconomic mills were gradually declining and the industry increasingly concentrated on the Lancashire coalfield. Taylor has summarised the available statistics to make the calculations shown in Table 5. The period from 1838 to 1850

TABLE 5

CHANGES IN LOCATION AND SOURCES OF POWER, 1838–50

	Variation in no. of factories	Decline in water power		Increase in steam power	
		h.p.	%	h.p.	%
Cheshire	−21	611	35	1,823	16
Derbyshire	−21	448	21	624	65
Lancashire	+49	182	5	17,001	57
Yorkshire	+54	158	11	2,559	143
Totals	+61	1,399	16	22,007	56

Source: A. J. Taylor, 'Concentration and Specialisation in the Lancashire Cotton Industry, 1825–1850', *Economic History Review*, 2nd ser., I (1948–9) 115.

coincides with that of the triumph of the power loom, an innovation that steadily drew the scattered colonies of hand-loom weavers into the mills – or offered them the prospect of indefinite unemployment. By 1833 almost every spinning mill at Stockport and Hyde had its weaving shed, and at Oldham combined firms were already in the majority. The further course of this process is summarised in Table 6, another of Taylor's tables. Again, the conclusion coincides with that of the last two

TABLE 6

INTEGRATION AND SPECIALISATION IN SPINNING AND
WEAVING, 1841–56

	Engaged solely in spinning	Engaged solely in weaving	Both processes	Total
1841 (all factories)	550	104	320	974
1841 (factories working)	475	88	293	856
1850	517	196	436	1,149
1856	591	344	516	1,451

Source: Taylor, loc. cit.

sections: that by the 1830s the increase in the optimum size of plant was squeezing out the smaller firms.

The statistics presented so far have serious deficiencies, quite apart from the question of reliability. In particular, the elementary method of estimation before 1834 excludes such major branches of the industry as calico printing, bleaching and dyeing, which were conducted in large capitalist enter-prises before spinning and weaving became mechanised, and it takes no account of emergent specialisms like machine building, heavy engineering (for water wheels, steam engines,transmission systems, etc.) and chemical production. Moreover, the statistics of the earlier period refer to fixed capital (i.e. invest-ment in building and plant), and take no account of working capital requirements, which were much larger in the earlier period.

Charles Wilson, in a stimulating exposition of 'The Entre-preneur in the Industrial Revolution in Britain', has shown that one of the most prominent features of the first phase of

34

industrialisation in Britain was the extension of the functions of the entrepreneur; the distinctive characteristic of the great figures of the Industrial Revolution, he writes, 'was that they fulfilled in one person the functions of capitalist, financier, works manager, merchant and salesman'.[27] We have already noticed the origins of this process in the early emergence of capitalist organisation in the finishing stages, where close supervision was most urgently needed, and have observed the merchants and country factors extending from the partial and uneven control characteristic of the domestic system to more direct control of the manufacturing process in the factory system. For the most successful, this proved to be only the beginning of a process that, in the early stages of rapid growth, brought direct control of almost all the manufacturing processes, and a range of service activities (such as transport and banking), under the immediate authority of the 'cotton lords'.[28]

The Industrial Revolution was an age of adventuring entrepreneurs and speculators, and the researcher regularly encounters much more heterogeneous and less manageable structures. Not infrequently, the existence of such firms is discovered in bankruptcy records and court cases. Thus Richard Paley, a Leeds soap-boiler who probably introduced cotton spinning on Arkwright's principles to the locality, not only had interests in a steam cotton mill at Leeds (Wilkinson, Holdforth & Paley) and three water-powered cotton mills at Colne, but was also a partner in ironworks at Wakefield and Bradford, and landlord of some 500 back-to-back tenements in Leeds, before his bankruptcy in 1803.[29] In Scotland, the legal framework was less restrictive and it was even more common for entrepreneurs with capital to become partners in a variety of enterprises. To take just once instance, Robert Dunmore, a merchant who became bankrupt in 1796, was not only founder of Ballindalloch cotton mill (1790), but also a partner in the Muirkirk Iron Works (1788), the Duntocher Wool Co. (1792),

[27] C. Wilson, 'The Entrepreneur in the Industrial Revolution in Britain', *History*, XLII (1957) p. 103.
[28] S. D. Chapman, 'The Peels in the Early English Cotton Industry', *Business History*, XI (1969) pp. 87–8.
[29] Chapman, 'The Cost of Power', pp. 15–16.

and an estate owner in Jamaica and Virginia.[30]

Such casualties, combined with the increasing complexity of the trade, inevitably pointed to the wisdom of more specialised and manageable firms,[31] but the process of disintegration was a hesitant one. In a fashion industry, specialisation could be a dangerous business policy, and in the course of growth many firms tried to extend the range of their functions – often, like the Peels, for adequate reasons, but sometimes as the consequence of uncontrolled ambition. Specialised branches of the industry, such as bleaching and machine building, are known to have existed from the 1770s, but this did not dissuade numbers of entrepreneurs from attempting to build up or maintain large integrated concerns.[32]

This sketch of the structure of the cotton industry draws attention to some of the features of the industry that frequently made the acquisition of capital and the maintenance of liquidity a serious problem. The numerous small firms, struggling to maintain a place in the industry, typically had few contacts outside a limited circle of friends, and found it difficult to obtain credit, while the hereditary leadership of merchant manufacturers was not sustained by the release of capital and broad profit margins for long after the turn of the century. Acquisition of landed property (initially for water-power rights) and the assumption of a wide range of functions brought numbers close to insolvency, or into the bankruptcy court, before the end of the eighteenth century.[33] To these

[30] J. R. Hume and John Butt, 'Muirkirk, 1788–1802: The Creation of a Scottish Industrial Community', *Scottish Historical Review*, XLV (1966) p. 167.

[31] M. M. Edwards, *The British Cotton Trade, 1780–1815* (Manchester, 1967) pp. 191, 234.

[32] Musson and Robinson, *Science and Technology in the Industrial Revolution*, esp. chaps. 8–10, 12–14; A. and N. Clow, *The Chemical Revolution* (1952) chaps. 8–12. For large integrated firms after 1850, see D. A. Farnie, 'The English Cotton Industry, 1850–96', unpublished M.A. thesis (Manchester, 1953) chap. 17.

[33] For case studies, see R. Boyson, *The Ashworth Cotton Enterprise* (Oxford, 1970); Unwin, *Samuel Oldknow*; and S. D. Chapman, 'James Longsdon, Farmer and Fustian Manufacturer', *Textile History*, I (3) (1970).

factors must be added the effects of war and commercial crises, particularly during the long period of the French Wars (1793–1815), which compelled prudent entrepreneurs to retain substantial and highly liquid reserves to meet any sudden and unexpected change in the economic situation. The commercial law of the period was not helpful, for the provisions of the Bubble Act of 1720 restricted the number of partners in an industrial or commercial enterprise to eight.

For most of the period covered by the present study, the provincial money market was evolving from very elementary beginnings, and entrepreneurs in need of capital drew on very diverse sources. The favourite source of capital was retained profits, and during the restricted growth period of Ark- wright's patents (1769–85) profit rates are known to have been very high; Robinsons of Nottingham, to take just one example, were earning 100 per cent on their investment in mills and plant in 1784. Even so, working capital requirements were so much larger than fixed capital, and the time-lag between de- cisions to build and profits so long, that financial difficulties could be experienced. 'I have been with Mr Robinson and he says . . . building etc. hath swallowed so much money that at present he sells [only] for ready cash', Thomas Oldknow wrote to his brother Samuel at Stockport in 1783.[34] Similarly, the first Sir Robert Peel said that in the early part of his career 'the greatest difficulty which he had to surmount was the want of capital to keep pace with his schemes of extension. The profits of the business were exceedingly great, and it admitted of great extension, but for some time the firm were hampered by the limited amount of their capital and credit.'[35] The correspondence of M'Connel & Kennedy, the Manchester leaders of the fine cotton-spinning industry, makes constant reference in the critical periods of the war years to the diffi- culties of raising money and to the reluctance of bankers to discount bills.[36] If the leaders of the industry suffered from

[34] Notts. C.R.O., DD 4P 79/63; Unwin, *Samuel Oldknow*, p. 13.
[35] Chapman, 'The Peels', p. 80.
[36] Edwards, *The British Cotton Trade*, p. 221.

intermittent financial strain, it cannot be expected that those who entered the industry after the years of abnormal profits, or who began with fewer connections, were insulated from such difficulties, and several other studies illustrate the financial problems of a variety of firms.[37]

Small firms that could not feed their own growth usually turned to their own families, and then to local business and social contacts for help. The law did not recognise shareholding in the modern sense until the Limited Liability Acts of 1855–6, but from the early part of the eighteenth century it became common for small businesses to borrow money on bond, and widows, clergymen, trustees, executors, retired tradesmen and other people with small savings were often glad to take advantage of this security. Small manufacturers might draw on the resources of a handful of local people who knew and trusted them, but this source of capital was not unfamiliar to much larger concerns. Cardwell, Birley & Hornby, the Blackburn cotton spinners, had ninety-seven small investors on their books in 1812, with a total investment of £36,000. In this instance, nearly all the loans were secured by a simple promise to pay, probably because the lenders were local people known personally to the partners.[38] In Scotland the legal framework was different; six, eight or ten partners in manufacturing concerns was already an established practice at the middle of the eighteenth century, and there was not the same need to draw on external sources.

However, sleeping partners were not uncommon in the English cotton industry, despite the risk of unlimited liability for the debts of the firm. Merchants were sometimes willing to enter into partnership with cotton manufacturers. A good example is provided by Gardom, Pares & Co. of Calver Bridge, near Sheffield, the partners in which consisted of representatives of the Heygate family, London hosiers and bankers, the Pares family, Leicester merchant hosiers, and the Gardoms,

<hr />

[37] e.g. J. Butt (ed.), *Robert Owen, Prince of Cotton Spinners* (Newton Abbot, 1971) chap. 7; Boyson, *The Ashworth Cotton Enterprise*, chap. 3.

[38] Edwards, *The British Cotton Trade*, pp. 255–7.

a line of Derbyshire hosiers that had become licensees of Arkwright in 1778.[39] Retired manufacturers would sometimes offer partnerships to promising young men, and a range of speculators entered the trade on similar terms, not infrequently to their loss. Improving landlords were often willing to provide or improve buildings for their tenantry, so that the cotton industry in Manchester and other parts of Lancashire owes something to the self-interest of the Earls of Derby, that of Glossop to the Duke of Norfolk, the Colne valley to Lord Dartmouth, and the Mansfield area (Notts.) to the Duke of Portland. In Glasgow the trading elite were intermarrying with the leading landowning families in Scotland in the second half of the eighteenth century, and partnerships to develop and exploit the best water-power sites in the country areas were common. Manufacturers fortunate enough to own land or buildings could readily mortgage them to raise capital or convert them to new uses.[40]

Other channels might be open to entrepreneurs who were seeking working capital. A survey of a variety of historical business records convinced Pollard that widespread encouragewas given to small manufacturers by the supplier merchants' habit of allowing four to eight months' credit, a sufficient period to work up the raw material and sell the product to wholesalers who, in some cases, might make advance payments in cash or bills of exchange.[41] The difficulty with such impressionistic judgements is that they rely on a wide range of records that may not be representative; certainly they are likely to neglect the kind of small entrepreneur whose pocketbook records have seldom survived. The early development of mercantile credit was certainly a factor in the growth of the cotton industry, but many of those who became manufac-

[39] M. H. MacKenzie, 'Calver Mill and Its Owners', *Derbyshire Archaeological Journal*, LXXXIII (1963).

[40] Edwards, *The British Cotton Trade*, pp. 195–8; for landlords, see, e.g., W. B. Crump and G. Ghorbal, *History of the Huddersfield Woollen Industry* (Huddersfield, 1935) pp. 77–8.

[41] S. Pollard, 'Fixed Capital in the Industrial Revolution in Britain', *Journal of Economic History*, XXIV (1964); Edwards, *The British Cotton Trade*, pp. 225–30.

turers were men of little education and few connections, and lived from hand to mouth. Authentic spokesmen from their ranks are difficult to find, but there is an occasional voice. Thus John Dugdale of the Lowerhouse Print Works, near Burnley, made some remarks in 1847 which, when translated from the vernacular, read: 'If you'll look back for the last six years, you'll find half of the printers are broken [bankrupt], and half of those that are left cannot break, for nobody will trust them; and the rest get on as well as they can.' A firm-by-firm survey of the Lancashire calico printers in 1846 confirms the impression of a preponderance of small and struggling entrepreneurs, with a high turnover of firms.[42]

London merchants and wholesale dealers also provided credit for northern manufacturers, but experience taught them to be highly selective. The spectacular bankruptcy in 1788 of Livesey, Hargreaves & Co. of Blackburn, the leading calico printers in the trade, was a severe setback to a number of London bankers. Samuel Oldknow, the early leader of the English muslin industry, was refused £5,000 credit by Saltes, his main London customers, in 1790. John Watson & Sons, the leading Preston cotton manufacturers, were more persuasive with their London customers, and at the time of their failure in 1809 had over £10,000 in credit from them.[43] These examples, and others which can be extracted from the records of the court of bankruptcy, show that the granting of credit was a risky business, even with the leading firms.

The rise of the mechanised cotton industry broadly coincided with that of country banking, and there is evidence of important connections between the two. The new banks saw their principal function as the provision of short-term loans (often on the security of buildings or land) and the discounting of bills of exchange. In some localities surviving bank records show that loan support to the cotton industry could be quite substantial. Thus in Nottingham, Smith, Payne & Smith, said to be the earliest bank in the provinces, advanced nearly

[42] G. Turnbull, *A History of Calico Printing in Great Britain* (Altrincham, 1951) pp. 73, 82.
[43] Unwin, *Samuel Oldknow*, p. 148; P.R.O., B1/124, p. 21.

£30,000 to ten cotton spinners in the peak building year of 1792, a figure which represented 30 per cent of Smith's total advances to its customers.[44] However, the formal establishment of banking in Nottingham anticipated that in Manchester by almost a century, and it seems that Lancashire cotton manufacturers did not enjoy such good facilities as those available in the East Midlands. Indeed, some leading manufacturers who (like Livesey, Hargreaves & Co.) drew directly on London banks, were forced to do so by the lack of credit facilities in Lancashire.

The main instrument of credit in Lancashire was the bill of exchange. The essential feature of the system was that the supplier of goods sent a bill to his customer for payment in anything from three to twelve months' time; the debtor accepted by signing and returning the bill, and the supplier might then pass on the endorsed bill to meet his own obligations, in effect using it as a medium of exchange like a bank note. Subsequent holders of the bill could make similar use of it, and frequent numbers of endorsements on surviving examples show that bills of exchange changed hands quite rapidly. The advantages and disadvantages of the system have been set out in a classic article by T. S. Ashton, 'The Bill of Exchange and Private Banks in Lancashire, 1790–1830'. It seems that the collapse of Livesey, Hargreaves & Co. in 1788 compelled several note-issuing banks to close their doors, and the widespread experience of loss produced a long-lasting antipathy to bank notes of all kinds. The bill of exchange, in contrast to the bank note, generally arose out of a specific transaction and so appeared 'to eighteenth-century minds to possess a stability that was often lacking in the promissory note of a mere banker. And, since each successive holder endorsed it, the more it circulated the greater the number of guarantors of its ultimate payment in cash.'[45] The confidence (however misplaced) that Lancashire gave to this system ensured an easy

[44] S. D. Chapman, *The Early Factory Masters* (Newton Abbot, 1967) pp. 139–41.
[45] T. S. Ashton and R. S. Sayers, *Papers in English Monetary History* (Oxford, 1953) p. 38.

41

and cheap system of credit for all the common transactions of everyday commerce. Numbers of banks were established in Lancashire by the end of the eighteenth century, but, compared with other parts of the country, relatively few of them issued notes.

4 *Commercial Organisation and Markets*

ALL the raw material used in the cotton industry was imported, and an organisation had to be evolved to supply the manufacturers with increasing quantities of raw cotton (or cotton wool, as it was generally known). From the early 1780s merchants and manufacturers recognised that further growth depended on increased supplies of cotton at low prices, particularly the finer qualities, and they were not slow to press their views with the Board of Trade and the planters. However, projects to increase the cotton crop in the West Indies (especially the Bahamas) and introduce the commodity into Sierra Leone met with only a limited response. The East India Company was reluctant to export the finer Indian staples as it was anxious to maintain its trade in Indian muslins, which depended on a restricted supply. The most encouraging response at first came from Brazil, where the crop was encouraged by the Portuguese Government, but this source was quickly superseded in the 1790s by the rapid expansion of cotton in the southern plantations of the recently established United States of America. In the early 1790s the profits on the cotton crop were high, and quickly displaced other cash crops, such as rice, indigo and tobacco. The supply of land seemed almost unlimited, particularly after the Louisiana purchase of 1801, and the United States cotton crop rose from 2 million lb. in 1791 to 182 million lb. in 1821, becoming the major source of Lancashire's supply at the turn of the century. The high elasticity of supply of cotton, due primarily to the responsiveness of the American planters and the adoption of Whitney's cotton gin, was clearly a crucial factor in the phenomenal growth of the British cotton industry in these years.[46]

The American planters were so successful in increasing the productivity of the cotton plantations, and the marketing machinery improved to such an extent, that after 1800 prices

[46] Edwards, *The British Cotton Trade*, chap. 5.

43

embarked on a course of more or less continuous decline. The United States Government's attempts to impose restrictions on exports in the period from December 1807 to May 1810 caused erratic fluctuations in prices at Liverpool, but did not affect the long-term trend. The elements of cost in the price of yarn can be illustrated from the data shown in Table 7. During the period of the French Wars, when it became

TABLE 7

ELEMENTS OF COST IN THE PRICE OF YARN, 1779–1812

Yarn 40 hanks to the lb. (roller spun)

	1779	1784	1799	1812
Selling price	16s. 0d.	10s. 11d.	7s. 6d.	2s. 6d.
Cost of cotton	2s. 0d.	2s. 0d.	3s. 4d.	1s. 6d.
Labour and capital	14s. 0d.	8s. 11d.	4s. 2d.	1s. 0d.

Yarn 100 hanks to the lb. (mule spun)

	1786	1796	1806	1812
Selling price	38s. 0d.	19s. 0d.	7s. 2d.	5s. 2d.
Cost of cotton	4s. 0d.	3s. 6d.	3s. 0d.	2s. 4d.
Labour and capital	34s. 0d.	15s. 6d.	4s. 2d.	2s. 10d.

Source: T. Ellison, *The Cotton Trade of Great Britain* (1886) p. 55.

more difficult to import wool from the Continent to supply the West Riding and other English manufacturers, the price of wool rose steeply, bringing an unexpected bonus to the cotton industry, and offering a further incentive to woollen and worsted manufacturers and merchants to turn over to cotton. The best price data available[47] can give little conception of the lament of England's old staple industry. As early as 1802 Robert Davison, a Nottingham hosier and spinner, complained that 'the high price of wool has produced a very great and alarming rivalry in cotton fabrics . . . the substitution of the latter for the former is immense . . . large mills and

[47] Ibid., p. 253; Rees, *Cyclopaedia*, article on 'Woollen Manufacture' (*c.* 1818).

factories originally destined to the working of woollens have been compelled to devote their works to cotton'.[48] In the West Riding, the displacement of worsteds by calicoes was at first amply compensated for by the rise of carpet making, upholstery, coach linings and other new branches, but by 1808 the Manchester trade dominated the Halifax and Colne areas and the upper Calder valley. The outcome was that the woollen and worsted industry, and not least the older centres in the West Country and East Anglia, suffered more reverses during the French Wars than did cotton.[49]

The organisation that evolved to market the cotton wool, the spun cotton yarns and cotton cloth was a complex one, and we can deal only with its salient features here. The need for numerous specialised functions can be readily appreciated from features of the industry that have already been noticed: the preponderance of small manufacturers, rapidly changing technology, considerable day-by-day fluctuations in market prices (sometimes due to war or commercial crisis, sometimes to capricious movements in fashion, and occasionally to unfounded rumour), and fairly widespread and regular shortages of capital. To these factors must be added slow and expensive communications, especially to the American, Indian and other distant markets, and the fact that the structure of commerce was slowly evolving for most of our period, certainly from 1780 to 1830. Much of what follows in the remainder of this section illustrates these features.

London was the principal port for cotton until at least 1795, and after that time London merchants and their agents were active in Liverpool, Manchester and other northern centres. Towards the end of the century Liverpool superseded London because most of the mills and workshops in the cotton industry were situated within sixty or eighty miles of the port, and had good canal and river connections with it. The rise of the United States as the major supplier of raw cotton was also an important factor. The cotton planter was separated from

[48] Quoted in Chapman, *The Early Factory Masters*, p. 215.
[49] Rees, *Cyclopaedia*, article on 'Cotton'. Cf. the decline of the Belfast linen industry at this period: E. R. R. Green, *The Lagan Valley, 1800–1850* (1949) chap. 4.

the mill owner by a range of specialised intermediaries; some big manufacturers tried to by-pass the system and deal directly with the growers, but commitment to any one source was found to be an unwise policy. The cotton wool was imported by ship-owning merchants or commission agents acting for the planter or exporter, often a British merchant resident in the United States. In the late eighteenth century the bags of imported cotton were bought up and distributed by Manchester cotton dealers, but these men were gradually superseded by the Liverpool cotton brokers, particularly after the opening of the Liverpool and Manchester railway (1830). Some of the brokers were offshoots of Liverpool merchant houses, but most of them migrated to the port from Manchester and the manufacturing districts. The successful broker combined knowledge of the needs of the industry (derived from his early experience in the mills and regular contacts with buyers) with daily intimacy with the cotton market and a reputation for 'strict probity and honour'. He needed capital, though many began their careers at Liverpool with slender financial resources. The fifty Manchester cotton dealers mentioned in a local directory of 1804 had been replaced by some ninety firms of Liverpool brokers in 1841, the year the Cotton Brokers' Association was formed. The cotton market at Liverpool was a highly competitive one, approximating to the economist's definition of a 'perfect market'. By constant circulation of samples and information bulletins (known as 'cotton circulars'), the brokers provided the 'perfect knowledge' necessary for the maintenance of this market.[50]

Williams shows that as the cotton trade expanded and became more sophisticated in its organisation and finance, the Liverpool family firms who had provided the enterprise for the eighteenth-century development of the port were augmented by branches of merchant houses from the United States, London and Glasgow. The number of merchants importing

[50] Edwards, *The British Cotton Trade*, chap. 6; T. Ellison, *The Cotton Trade of Great Britain* (1886) esp. part II, chap. 3; F. E. Hyde, B. B. Parkinson and S. Marriner, 'The Cotton Broker and the Rise of the Liverpool Cotton Market', *Economic History Review*, 2nd ser., VIII (1955–6).

cotton into Liverpool in any one year ran into hundreds, but a large proportion of the trade was handled by a small group of some thirty operators who specialised in the import of cotton, mostly from the United States alone.[51]

In discussing the structure of the industry, we have already examined the trend towards disintegration that set in at an early stage of expansion. Vertically integrated firms like Peels, Arkwrights and Douglases were exceptional even in their day, and their relative importance appears to have declined. The existence of a large number of small firms specialising in carding and spinning gave rise to another specialised market, that for yarns. The larger spinners, like Strutts of Belper and M'Connel & Kennedy of Manchester, had selling agents in all the markets – Glasgow, Belfast, Nottingham and other centres – constantly instructing them on prices for the different yarn counts. The smaller spinners were usually dependent on yarn merchants or brokers, who allowed them cotton wool on credit and bought up their small consignments. Here, as elsewhere, the market was a highly competitive one, and those with little capital depended on the favour of merchants and were most vulnerable to sudden changes in demand.[52]

Edwards shows that between 1780 and 1815 the market for cotton cloth continued to be centred on London, but that the period saw a decisive shift of the focus of trade towards Manchester. Though a few outstanding northern firms like the Peels of Manchester and I. & R. Morley, the Nottingham hosiers, opened their own warehouses in London before the end of the century, the London tradesmen's more ready access to capital and their close contact with fashion movements contrived to tie provincial merchants and manufacturers to them. There appear to have been three common types of connection between the centre of trade and the centres of manufacturing. Some firms in the provinces had a partner

[51] D. M. Williams, 'Liverpool Merchants and the Cotton Trade, 1820–1850', in J. R. Harris (ed.), *Liverpool and Merseyside* (1969).

[52] C. H. Lee, 'Marketing Organisation and Policy in the Cotton Trade: M'Connel & Kennedy', *Business History*, x (1968); Fitton and Wadsworth, *The Strutts and the Arkwrights*, chap. 11; Edwards, *The British Cotton Trade*, chap. 7.

in London or a working agreement with a London merchant, and this close personal connection was particularly important in fashion lines like calico printing and hosiery. Other goods from the provinces were handled by commission agents who sold by private contract or at weekly public sales, or by warehousemen who bought goods outright from the provincial manufacturers. Unwin's *Samuel Oldknow and the Arkwrights* provides some fascinating insights into the ways a London buyer could advise a manufacturer on market requirements and encourage him to improve his product, take up new lines and drop more traditional ones.

The emergence of Manchester as the international emporium for cotton goods can be traced to a number of developments around the turn of the century. The necessity for keeping a warehouse or stockroom in Manchester soon spread beyond the Lancashire manufacturing region. In the 1790s Midlands and West Riding cotton spinners were maintaining stocks for sale in the town, and the Scots soon learned that it saved time to meet drapers there rather than travel the country towns for small orders. London warehousemen found it an advantage to keep an agent posted at the centre of manufacturing. A growing concourse of country drapers was drawn to the street markets and inns to scramble for bargains, or to jostle at the counters of the increasing numbers of warehouses. Some idea of the rapidity of growth of trade is indicated by the number of warehouses in the town, which leaped from 120 in 1772 to 726 in 1820 and 955 in 1829, though many of these would be converted tenements in the original warehouse district in and around Cannon Street and High Street.[53]

In the train of provincial manufacturers and London warehousemen came overseas merchants. The technical advances of the later eighteenth century were quickly sought out by the French Government, who soon had English artisans working in their country. 'You can keep a secret in a German factory, because the workers are obedient, prudent, and satis-

[53] Edwards, *The British Cotton Trade*, pp. 172–4; R. Smith, 'Manchester as a Centre for Manufacturing and Merchanting of Cotton Goods, 1820–30', *University of Birmingham Historical Journal*, IV (1953–4).

fied with a little; but the English workers are insolent, quarrelsome, adventurous and greedy for money. It is never difficult to seduce them from their employment', the French minister Calonne declared in 1788.[54] Scattered accounts of the careers of English artisans who went abroad suggest that several showed similar personality traits in their dealings with European firms and governments, and not infrequently cost their hosts much expense and trouble with little benefit.[55] The French Revolution and the French Wars dislocated trade severely, and hampered the illegal migration of men and machinery across the Channel, so that it was not until the 1830s that French and Belgian textile technology showed signs of catching up with the British, while the Germans and other Continental countries were even further behind. One consequence was that increasing numbers of German, Dutch, Swiss, French and Italian merchants were drawn to Manchester, and after 1835 they were followed by Greeks, Spaniards, Portuguese, Russians and other traders.[56]

The presence of this large colony of Continental merchants in Manchester must not be taken as indicative of British merchants' lack of interest in the export market. We have already noticed the existence of a vigorous export trade to Africa, America and France at the middle of the eighteenth century. The point here is to attempt to identify the kind of organisation that was developed to sustain the growth of the overseas market. N. S. Buck's *Development of the Organisation of the Anglo-American Trade, 1800–1850* shows that British merchants and manufacturers dominated the trade with the United States until at least 1830. He maintains that up to the end of the French Wars (1815) British export merchants, often supported

[54] Lévy-Leboyer, *Les Banques Européennes*, p. 25.

[55] See, e.g., J. Voortman, *Les Débuts de l'Industrie Cotonnière* . . . (Ghent, 1940) pp. 323–4; C. Ballot, *L'Introduction du Machinisme dans l'Industrie Française* (Lille and Paris, 1923) *passim*; A. L. van Schelven, 'De Dixons op het Continent', *Textielhistorische Bijdragen*, no. 12 (1970).

[56] Lévy-Leboyer, *Les Banques Européennes*, pp. 510–16; S. Pollard and C. Holmes, *Documents of European Economic History*, I (1968) 285–94.

by one of the large Anglo-American banking houses in London, conducted most of the trade across the North Atlantic, though a few American importers had branches in Britain, and some British manufacturers were beginning to assume mercantile functions. In the next fifteen years the manufacturer overtook the merchant as the most active figure in the export trade, and it was not until after 1830 that the American importer became an important figure in the commerce of the North Atlantic. However, it must be borne in mind that this analysis is concerned with the whole range of American imports and exports, and developments in cotton, which was perhaps the most advanced sector of the economy, may have preceded those in other sectors; that is to say, some manufacturers may have taken to exporting before 1815. Edwards's work certainly gives this impression, but it would hardly have been possible without bank or merchant credit, as American importers demanded at least twelve months' credit. The history of a small firm exporting to Russia in the early years of the century reveals that a year's credit was also required in St Petersburg, which was a source of great financial strain on the partners.[57]

A similar problem of intermittent financial difficulties in supplying a distant market is conveyed by a recent study of a Glasgow firm of muslin manufacturers who were active in the Indian market towards the end of our period. John Lean & Sons was established in 1840 and shortly came to specialise in the Calcutta market. Slaven concludes:

Often the production of goods was carried on in substantial ignorance of the real capacity of the markets, and sometimes in direct conflict with advice received from representatives on the spot. The changes in taste, frequently occurring with bewildering speed and compounded by the insurmountable delays in the transmission of news, highlighted the inflexibility of a manufacturing policy which attempted to meet the market with long runs of standard patterns and

[57] N. S. Buck, *Development of the Organisation of the Anglo-American Trade, 1800–1850* (1925) chaps. 5–8; Edwards, *The British Cotton Trade*, pp. 89–97; Chapman, 'James Longsdon', pp. 274–5.

goods. With a manufacturing policy repeatedly out of step with current market demands, a slow turnover of stock was almost inevitable.[58]

In this, as in the case of so many other business histories, it is impossible to know how representative the firm was. The most that can be said is that the modest experience and capital of the partners was fairly typical, and the physical problems of communication faced all firms until the coming of the telegraph.

Unfortunately, there are no comparable studies of firms trading to the Continent to illuminate the structure and problems of that particular market. It is said that English manufacturers and merchants were at first reluctant to send travellers abroad, and if this is true it offers some explanation of the deficiency of historical evidence on sales organisation in the European market. Until the end of the eighteenth century the great European fairs at Beaucaire (near Mulhouse), Leipzig, Frankfurt and Salerno retained their traditional status in the textile trade, and their role continued to be important up to the railway age. Lancashire merchant-manufacturers like Samuel Oldknow and William Radcliffe traded through these fairs in the 1790s, but during the Napoleonic Wars Kirkman Finlay (the leading Glasgow merchant) and M'Connel & Kennedy (the Manchester pioneers of fine cotton spinning) learned to by-pass the old organisation by direct trade with Continental agents. Furture research will probably show that other firms followed their lead.[59]

Statistics are available to indicate the relative importance of the various export markets from 1780 to 1850. Up to the end of the French Wars the outstanding feature was the rapid growth of sales of cotton piece goods and yarn to North America,

[58] A. Slaven, 'A Glasgow Firm in the Indian Market: John Lean & Sons, Muslin Weavers', *Business History Review*, XLIII (1969).

[59] C. Fohlen, *L'Industrie Textile au Temps du Second Empire* (Paris, 1956) pp. 148–9; *James Finlay & Co. Ltd, 1750–1950* (Glasgow, 1951) pp. 7, 15, 18; C. H. Lee, *A Cotton Enterprise, 1795–1840: A History of M'Connel & Kennedy, Fine Cotton Spinners* (Manchester, 1972) chap. 4.

Europe and the West Indies, though war-time dislocations caused substantial changes from one year to another as one market closed and another was opened. Analysis of sales by country of destination is not a very fruitful exercise because there was a large volume of entrepôt trade abroad, especially through the fairs of Italy and Germany, and through American ports like New York and Boston. Around the turn of the century cottons edged out woollens to become the most important British export, and by the end of the Napoleonic Wars they represented 40 per cent of the total income from exports. They fluctuated around this level until mid-century, despite a more or less continuous decline in prices.[60]

Exports to Europe and North America continued to increase in the first half of the nineteenth century, but as a proportion of total exports they fell quite sharply. The introduction of the American tariff in 1815 and the removal of British restrictions on the export of machinery in 1843 are benchmarks in this relative decline, but industrialisation of the more advanced countries was the underlying cause. By contrast, the share of the underdeveloped countries increased dramatically. India took only 0·5 per cent of British cotton cloth exports in 1815, but this figure advanced by leaps and bounds from the middle 1830s, reaching 23 per cent in 1850 and 31 per cent in 1860. Other parts of the Orient, South America, the West Indies and Africa also increased their shares. The trend was accompanied by an overall deterioration in the quality of cloth produced, a development that augured badly for the long-term future of the industry.[61]

[60] Edwards, *The British Cotton Trade*, chap. 4; A. Imlah, *Economic Elements in the Pax Britannica* (Cambridge, Mass., 1958) esp. pp. 103–7.

[61] Ellison, *The Cotton Trade of Great Britain*, pp. 63–4; L. G. Sandberg, 'Movements in the Quality of British Cotton Textile Exports', *Journal of Economic History*, xxviii (1968).

5 Labour and Industrial Relations

IN approaching the problems of recruitment of labour and of industrial relations, it is convenient to make an initial distinction between factory and domestic labour. Increasing quantities of cotton goods at falling prices was responsible for increases in the numbers of men, women and juveniles employed in both categories for most of the period covered by this study, but in almost all other respects the characteristics of the labour force in the two sectors were quite different. They must therefore be considered separately, while recognising the important links between them.

The main problem in recruiting a factory labour force was the reluctance of workers to enter the mills, particularly in the country areas where even large workshops were unfamiliar. Arkwright had no difficulty in filling his Manchester mill in 1783 – indeed he had so many applications that he had to turn good families away – but eight miles away, at Styal, the Gregs had to scrape together a labour force from the country round about and from more distant workhouses.[62] Similar contrasts can be drawn between the experience of mill owners in Nottingham and Glasgow and those in the respective country areas,[63] with the proviso that the first major factory enterprise in the smaller towns might soak up the entire available labour supply. When Charles Hulbert opened a cotton mill at Shrewsbury in 1803, he found that his main difficulty was to recruit a labour force, because 'the great linen mills of Messrs Marshall, Benyon and Bage had taken the lead and the great portion of young people willing to be employed in manufactories were engaged'. Moreover, Hulbert explained, young people in agricultural areas (where the mill owners were forced to resort

[62] F. Collier, *The Family Economy of the Working Classes in the Cotton Industry* (Manchester, 1965) p. 14.
[63] Chapman, *The Early Factory Masters*, pp. 164–8; for Scotland, cf. David Dale's need to employ pauper apprentices at New Lanark, twenty-three miles from Glasgow: Butt (ed.), *Robert Owen*, pp. 188–95.

for water power) were slower to learn, and 'many of our instructed workpeople, notwithstanding all were engaged at regular wages for three years, left us for Manchester, Stockport, etc. . . . We soon found that if business must be carried on to any great extent where hand labour was required, it must be in the neighbourhood of like manufactories, where an advance of wages would speedily obtain the number of hands required.'[64]

The mill owners' problem can only be understood by examining the recruitment of skilled workers (machine builders, millwrights and mule spinners) separately from that of the unskilled machine minders who formed the majority of the labour force in Arkwright-type mills. The fundamental difficulty in obtaining skilled men was simply the consequence of the rapid growth of the cotton industry, which made artisans with relevant skills very much at a premium. Local newspaper advertisements, memoirs, private correspondence and high wage rates all bear testimony to the acute shortage of craftsmen whose skills could be applied to textile machine building or to the installation of water wheels and transmission systems.

The aversion of unskilled labour to employment in cotton mills largely stemmed from dislike of long, uninterrupted shifts in the mill (agricultural and domestic labour was generally more intermittent), and from the similarity of the early factories to the parish workhouses. The comparison often made between the two was not so much a question of architecture, or of the stigma attached to workhouse labour, so much as the insistence in both on close and continuous supervision of work by overseers. The consequence of this popular repugnance to factory life was that employment in the mills often represented casual labour for those who, for the time being, could find nothing better, and as late as the 1830s Samuel Greg regarded the 'restless and migratory spirit' of his mill workers as one of the main problems which troubled him as an employer.[65]

The literature on labour in the early factory system is very largely an examination of the techniques that were used to

[64] C. Hulbert, *Memoirs of Seventy Years of an Eventful Life* (1852), p. 195.
[65] A. Redford, *Labour Migration in England, 1800–50* (1926) chap. 2.

recruit and retain a work-force, and the varying responses to them. The obvious solution, as Hulbert concluded, was to offer better wage rates than one's competitors, and factory wages quickly rose above those offered to agricultural labourers and to workers in domestic industry; by 1834 it was claimed (without contradiction) that 'The wages in the cotton factories of Lancashire are the best in England', while 'the poor's rate is lower than in any other manufacturing district'.[66] However, experience soon showed that big wage packets were not the only solution, particularly where it was necessary to attract workers to isolated mill sites. At Cromford, Arkwright found it necessary to offer employment to whole families, and to build houses before they could be induced to move from Nottingham, Derby or Manchester. By 1790 he was providing a public house, a weekly market and garden allotments to retain his work-force.[67] The Strutts at Belper, David Dale at New Lanark, the Evanses at Darley Abbey, the Gregs at Styal, and other factory colony builders had to offer comparable incentives, but, like Arkwright, they found that the establishment of a new community was an expensive and often frustrating experience, and labour turnover continued at a very high rate.[68]

The remoter mills were unable to collect a labour force even by advertising, and had to have recourse to the workhouse for their unskilled workers. The late eighteenth century was a period of rapid population growth, and many of the workhouses of London and the southern counties were glad to send consignments of pauper children to the northern mills for an apprenticeship of anything from a year to eight years, depending on their age. The pauper apprenticeship system has often been discussed in terms of exploitation of juvenile labour, and there can be no doubt that the children worked long

[66] Collier, *The Family Economy*, p. 47, n. 3.
[67] Fitton and Wadsworth, *The Strutts and the Arkwrights*, pp. 246–60.
[68] Butt (ed.), *Robert Owen*, pp. 188–95; Jean Lindsay, 'An Early Industrial Community: The Evans Cotton Mill at Darley Abbey, 1783–1810', *Business History Review*, xxxiv (1960); Collier, *The Family Economy*, pp. 39–43.

hours for abysmal wages. But the few records of the system that have survived show that the apprenticeship system was not as cheap as free labour. It was in any case short-lived, partly because as the first generation of apprentices grew to adulthood the colony became self-perpetuating, but more especially because after the turn of the century the Arkwright-type mills were giving way to mule spinning factories, for which the availability of water power was a less important factor in location.[69]

Having collected and housed his labour force, the factory master's problems were by no means over. He had to train his machine operatives and, what was much more difficult, to induce them to become willing, obedient, regular, punctual and sober servants of his company. The most successful entrepreneurs of the Industrial Revolution were those who succeeded in imposing their system of work discipline on their labour force, and the cotton industry nurtured two or three of the outstanding figures in this small group of men of iron determination. Arkwright, according to the earliest informed account of his activities, introduced into every department of the cotton manufacture 'a system of industry, order and cleanliness, till then unknown in any manufactory where great numbers were employed together, but which he so effectually accomplished that his example may be regarded as the origin of almost all similar improvement'.[70] Like Arkwright, the first Sir Robert Peel 'introduced among his operatives that order, arrangement and sub-division of employment which form the marked characteristics of the factory system . . . he insisted on a system of punctuality and regularity which approached the discipline of military drill'.[71]

Pollard has analysed the methods that were used to institute and maintain this new regimen.[72] The most common deterrents were corporal punishment (for juveniles), fines for breaking the factory rules, and the threat of dismissal. However, the

[69] Chapman, *The Early Factory Masters*, pp. 169–71; Collier, *The Family Economy*, p. 45.
[70] Rees, *Cyclopaedia*, article on 'Cotton'.
[71] Chapman, 'The Peels', p. 72.
[72] S. Pollard, *The Genesis of Modern Management* (1965), chap. 5.

history of industrial relations in the industry shows that workers were not always easily intimidated, and James Montgomery's *Carding and Spinning Master's Assistant* (1832) advised that 'operatives are generally unwilling to submit to fines either for bad work or improper conduct; it seems to be a general feeling amongst them that they would much rather have the master turn them away than fine them'.[73] Incentives, notably some system of payment by results, were also widely used. The third method, comprehensible only in the light of the employers' need to establish a novel pattern of work on a large scale, was the attempt to inculcate in the workers the mill owners' own set of values and priorities. The ultimate aspiration of the mill owner for his workpeople can be seen in the Strutts' boast of their success in bringing sober and industrious habits to Belper.[74] The manufacturing squires at factory colonies like Belper had virtual control of the whole of the local population, but their authority must not be exaggerated. Boyson's recent study of the Ashworths of Turton (a factory colony near Bolton) portrays two brothers with a messianic sense of the cotton manufacturers' destiny as the nation's spirit of enterprise and social conscience, but adds that their employees 'accepted the social and moral standards set by the Ashworths, but politically their views were their own'.[75]

The early nineteenth-century literature on the cotton industry has distorted our view of the industry by giving undue prominence to the factory colonies; influential works like Dr J. P. Kay's *Condition of the Working Classes employed in the Cotton Manufacture in Manchester* (1832) and W. Cooke Taylor's *Notes of a Tour in the Manufacturing Districts of Lancashire* (1841) saw the model factory colony as the ideal arrangement of industrial society. But, as we have already noted, the factory colony had reached its meridian by the turn of the century, and at the end of the French Wars the urban mule spinning mills had become the predominant form of enterprise; Bolton was

[73] Montgomery, *Carding and Spinning Master's Assistant*, p. 222; cf. A. Aspinall, *The Early English Trade Unions* (1949) p. 364.

[74] *Select Committee on Children employed in Manufactories, Parliamentary Papers* (1816) III p. 217.

[75] Boyson, *The Ashworth Cotton Enterprise*, p. 135.

much more typical of the industry than Belper. Mule spinners have already been mentioned as one of the grades of artisans whose skills were very much at a premium, and their position in the structure of industrial relations must now be examined more closely. Mule spinning, as we saw in Section 2, was only mechanised slowly, and even when the automatic mule became widely adopted (after about 1835), the spinner retained his quasi-independent status. A generation after the period covered by this book, the finest spinning still depended on the sensitive touch of the mule spinner, while spinners of the medium and coarser yarns successfully contrived to introduce individuality to their machines. Catling explains that 'every operative spinner was firmly of the opinion that no two mules could ever be made alike. As a consequence he proceeded to tune and adjust each of his own particular pair of mules with little respect for the intentions of the maker or the principles of engineering. Before very long, no two mules ever were alike . . . [and] it was usually unwise to move a spinner about other than in exceptional circumstances.'[76]

All the available wage statistics confirm that the mule spinner was the best-paid artisan in the cotton industry (apart from overlookers) throughout the period covered by this study.[77] In the mill, he enjoyed semi-independent status, was paid on piece-rates, employed his own assistants (one or two 'piecers' for each mule) and owed responsibility only to the spinner-room overlooker, who was (with the engineer, the carder and the warehouseman) answerable to the general manager. The accounts of a typical small warp and mule spinning mill of the mid-1830s, employing forty people, show that the four mule spinners and their piecers took half of the weekly wage bill of £24. Outside the mill, his status in the community was recognised by the best rooms in some public houses being marked 'Mule Spinners Only'. The mule spinners maintained their own trade unions, the Manchester one well established in 1795, and those in other centres apparently close on its heels. By 1815 the mule spinners' unions,

[76] Catling, *The Spinning Mule*, pp. 118, 149.

[77] e.g. Baines, *History of the Cotton Manufacture*, pp. 436, 438, 442–3, 445.

58

together with those of the calico printers, impressed the employers as a 'most formidable' group of militant organisations which they had to reckon with.[78]

In Section 2 we saw that carding and spinning became factory processes some thirty or forty years before weaving, and the consequence was an ever-increasing demand for handloom weavers, many of whom had to be recruited further and further afield from the old centres of the cotton industry. Cardwell, Birley & Hornby, the Blackburn merchants and spinners, increased their weavers from 132 in 1777 to 770 in 1788; at the other extremity of the Lancashire region, William Radcliffe was distributing warps to weavers up to thirty miles from Mellor, on the Pennine side of Stockport. By the end of the century Sir Robert Peel had fifteen depots as far apart as Blackburn in the north, Stockport in the south, Chapel-en-le-Frith (Derbyshire) to the east, and Walton (Liverpool) to the west. Very often the growth points were no more than a mile or two out of town, as surviving loomhouses on the Pennine scarp above Oldham and Rochdale show, but in other instances villages at a distance from the established urban centres were suddenly brought to new prosperity by migrating capital. Burnley, for instance, became a major centre of the cotton industry when several Bolton merchant-manufacturers 'began to employ a great number of weavers and spinners in the cotton branch'. Similarly, the skills of the muslin weavers of Paisley induced Peels, Arkwrights and other Lancashire cotton firms to invest capital in developments there, and so successful was this partnership that when John Marshall (the Leeds flax spinner) visited Scotland in 1803, he maintained that Manchester fine spinning and Paisley production of fine fabrics were the two complementary branches of the cotton industry.[79]

Bythell's important study of *The Handloom Weavers* shows the

[78] Catling, *The Spinning Mule*, chaps. 9–10; J. Montgomery, *Theory and Practice of Cotton Spinning* (1836) pp. 251–2; N. Smelser, *Social Change in the Industrial Revolution* (1959) pp. 318–19; Aspinall, *The Early English Trade Unions*, p. 214.

[79] S. D. Chapman, Introduction to G. J. French, *The Life and Times of Samuel Crompton* (1859; new ed., 1970) p. vi.

TABLE 8

ESTIMATES OF THE NUMBERS OF DOMESTIC WORKERS
IN THE COTTON INDUSTRY, 1795–1833

	Handloom weavers (cotton only)	Auxiliaries	Framework knitters	
1795	75,000[a]	15,000[b]	1782	20,000[c]
1811	225,000[a]	45,000[b]	1812	29,600[c]
1833	250,000[b]	50,000[b]	1844	48,500[c]

Sources: [a]G. J. French, *The Life and Times of Samuel Crompton* (1859; new ed., 1970) pp. 275–8.

[b]D. Bythell, *The Handloom Weavers* (1969) pp. 54–7, 86.

[c]Hosiery statistics most conveniently summarised in D. M. Smith, 'The British Hosiery Industry at the Middle of the Nineteenth Century', *Transactions of the Institute of British Geographers*, xxxi (1963) 129.

difficulties of acquiring reliable estimates of the total number of cotton weavers before 1833, but it is possible to calculate the order of magnitude (see Table 8). In 1811, G. A. Lee and Thomas Ainsworth conducted a census of mule spinning and concluded that it employed 150,000 weavers and was responsible for two-thirds of the output of the industry. The other third obviously came from the sector operating Arkwright's technique and, *pro rata*, must have found employment for 75,000 weavers, making 225,000 in all. Until the mid-1790s the mule sector was still very small, and after that time the Arkwright sector ceased to grow, so that 75,000 cotton weavers would approach a fair estimate for 1795. These figures are consistent with abundant literary evidence of the rapid growth of handloom weaving from around 1780 to the end of the French Wars. The number of domestic framework knitters also multiplied, but unfortunately there are no statistics to distinguish cotton frames from those engaged on knitting wool, silk and linen. The number of workers in the domestic sector of the cotton industry may be compared with 220,000 employed in nearly 1,200 mills in Great Britain and Ireland in 1833.[80] Clearly, the number of domestic workers exceeded the number of factory workers until at least the middle 1830s,

[80] Baines, *History of the Cotton Manufacture*, p. 394.

when the power loom won the confidence of the mill owners.

The dispersion of the handloom weavers over a large part of Lancashire and the adjacent parts of Cheshire, Derbyshire and the West Riding, as well as the Glasgow–Paisley area, prevented them from uniting to defend their living standards, and their protracted capitulation to the power loom constitutes one of the most miserable chapters of social history. Inevitably, such pathos has attracted a great deal of writing and a variety of interpretations, often flavoured by the political presuppositions of the contributors to the debate. Most recently, Bythell, and Thompson's *The Making of the English Working Class*, have offered sharply contrasting explanations of the significance of the downward trend of weavers' incomes after the French Wars. Thompson sees self-employed weavers, yeoman weavers and journeyman weavers all thrust down into the same debased proletariat,[81] while Bythell maintains that by 1815 cotton handloom weaving had largely become an unskilled and casual occupation which provided part-time work for women and children, a reservoir of labour that was accustomed to flow into varying channels with the changing seasons and state of trade. While admitting that 'there was terrible suffering in some districts in the 1820s, 1830s, and early 1840s' (particularly in fringe areas like Burnley, Colne and Padiham, where few new mills were being built or equipped with power looms), Bythell thinks that 'most of the handloom weavers in the cotton industry were absorbed into alternative employment with remarkable speed and ease'.[82] This divergence of views, both depending on incomplete evidence, can only be evaluated when we have the benefit of more local studies, particularly those founded on parish registers and the census enumerators' returns of 1841, 1851 and 1861. In the meantime, the only safe comment that can be made is that the standards of living of workers in the cotton industry, like those in the economy at large, show a bewildering variety of contrasts, not only between occupations, but over periods of time and between different localities.

[81] E. P. Thompson, *The Making of the English Working Class* (1963) esp. pp. 270–1.

[82] Bythell, *The Handloom Weavers*, p. 271.

6 The Role of Cotton in the Growth of the Economy

THE period between about 1450 and 1750 saw relatively few mechanical inventions introduced into the European textile industries; the stocking frame at the end of the sixteenth century and the Dutch loom in the seventeenth appear to be the only conspicuous exceptions to this generalisation. The great burst of invention that began with Arkwright and Crompton has some roots reaching down earlier in the century, but the desultory reception of Kay's flying shuttle and Lewis Paul's roller spinning in the 1730s and 1740s occurred in a different economic climate from the last thirty years of the century. Most of the explanations that are offered on the causes of this unprecedented period of technical development have been familiar to historians for a long time: a chronic shortage of yarn and steeply rising costs as weavers adopting the flying shuttle had to draw their yarn supplies from domestic spinners further and further away; the physical qualities of cotton, which make it peculiarly amenable to mechanical handling; and the high elasticity of supply of raw cotton from the rapidly growing United States.

The growing consumption of cotton must have been initiated by an increase in demand, and on this point Professor Eversley provides some help. Eversley postulates that between 1750 and 1780 the number of households in the middle income range (£50 to £400 p.a.) rose from 15 per cent of the population of England to 20 or even 25 per cent. In Eversley's model the foundation of the Industrial Revolution was laid by the sale of articles of everyday life to this 'middle class' of consumers.[83] Cotton fits well into this thesis in the middle decades of the eighteenth century in so far as the widespread and growing sale of linen mixtures and printed goods largely issued from this sector of the population, and formed the basis from

[83] D. E. C. Eversley, 'The Home Market and Economic Growth in England, 1750–80', in E. L. Jones and G. E. Mingay (eds.), *Land, Labour and Population in the Industrial Revolution* (1967).

which sales of cheaper machine-spun and printed cottons accelerated after about 1780.

The role of cotton in the British economy in the last two decades of the eighteenth century has been the subject of lively debate following the publication of Rostow's 'take-off' theory of economic growth. Searching for a framework in which to set the evolution of modern industrial societies, he suggested that there were five stages of economic growth: the traditional society, the satisfaction of preconditions for 'take-off', the 'take-off', the drive to maturity, and the age of high mass consumption. In Rostow's words, 'the "take-off" consists, in essence, of the achievement of rapid growth in a limited group of sectors, where modern industrial techniques are applied'. He identified cotton textiles as the leading sector in 'take-off' in Britain, and defined the take-off period as 1783–1802, citing the spectacular increase in the import of raw cotton in the decades 1781–91 (319 per cent) and 1791–1801 (67 per cent) as his empirical support.[84]

The idea of cotton making the decisive advance that impelled the whole economy forward into rapid industrial growth is evidently a bold one, and provoked critical examination by a number of economists and historians, particularly by Phyllis Deane and W. A. Cole. They calculated that it is unlikely that cotton contributed more than 5 per cent of the British national income by the end of Rostow's take-off period (see Table 9). The figure (assuming for a moment that it is correct) demonstrates that cotton was already making an impressive contribution to the economy. But Habakkuk and Deane also calculated that iron was making an equivalent contribution to the economy at the period, and if their figures are accepted it is difficult to understand how cotton alone can be labelled *the* leading sector.[85]

However, Deane and Cole's estimates of the value of the output of the cotton industry are admitted to be 'highly tentative', and any calculation of its contribution to British

[84] W. W. Rostow, *The Stages of Economic Growth* (1960).

[85] H. J. Habakkuk and P. Deane, 'The Take-off in Britain', in W. W. Rostow (ed.), *The Economics of Take-off into Sustained Growth* (1965) p. 71.

TABLE 9

ESTIMATES OF THE OUTPUT OF THE COTTON INDUSTRY AND ITS CONTRIBUTION TO
NATIONAL INCOME, 1760–1817

Years	(1) Retained imports (£m.)	(2) Gross value of output (£m.)	(3) Multiplier (2) ÷ (1)	(4) Value added (£m.) (2)−(1)	(5) National income (£m.)	(6) Value added as % of national income
1760	0·2	0·6	3·0	0·4		
1772–4	0·2	0·9	4·5	0·6		
1781–3	1·0	4·0	4·0	2·0	c. 160	c. 1%
1784–6	1·6	5·4	3·4	3·8		
1787–9	2·3	7·0	3·0	4·7		
1795–7	2·6	10·0	4·0	7·4		
1798–1800	5·7	11·1	2·0	5·4		
1801–3	4·0	15·0	3·7	11·0	230	4–5%
1805–7	4·5	18·9	4·2	14·4		
1811–13	5·3	28·3	5·3	23·0	301	7–8%
1815–17	8·3	30·0	3·7	21·7		

Source: P. Deane and W. A. Cole, *British Economic Growth 1688–1959* (Cambridge, 1967) Table 42, pp. 185, 188 (simplified). Col. (3) inserted by present author (see text).

national income must be even more hazardous. These calculations depend on a sequence of estimates extracted from the controversial pamphlet literature of the period (see Table 9, col. (2)). The best that can be said for them is that they appear to have been synthesised from statistics of the value of retained imports (i.e. imports minus re-exports), but Table 9, col. (3), shows that the different estimators multiplied these figures by anything from 2·0 to 5·3, an inconsistency that hints strongly at the possibility of error. The value of the imported raw material was more than doubled at the spinning stage (see Table 7, p. 44), and one suspects that the estimates used by Deane and Cole neglect value added at the bleaching, dyeing and (above all) printing stages. Peels, the leading printers at the end of the eighteenth century, sold their rolls at £4 to £5 each, but it seems they were worth only £1·30 as white calico.[86]

The possible errors in Table 9 can be illustrated in another way. Their estimate for 1798–1800 may appear to be an exception to my remarks about the limitations of Deane and Cole's figures for gross output, as it was made by Eden for the Globe Insurance Company. Eden's original figure was £10 million, but the previous year the secretaries of the Sun Fire Office, Royal Exchange and Phoenix insurance companies procured information 'from cotton spinners and from an engineer who has built many mills' and calculated that the value of the output of the industry 'amounts to about £20 million'. The difference between the two estimates can be explained by the London insurance companies' determination to take note of bleach and printing works.[87] In 1834 capital invested in the finishing trades was equal to half that in spinning and weaving (see Table 4, p. 31), and though there is no direct relationship between capital invested and value of output, it is reasonable to recognise this as a further indication of the importance of bleaching, dyeing and printing. Until more is known about the finishing trades it is not possible to be too emphatic, but it seems that Deane and Cole's figures may underestimate the

[86] Chapman, 'The Peels', p. 86.
[87] Chatham papers, P.R.O., 30/8/187.

contribution of the industry to the gross national product. If £20 million is a realistic estimate of gross value of output in 1797, value added was £17 million, and cotton was already contributing over 7 per cent of the national income.

As far as the study of the British cotton industry is concerned, the most suggestive part of the Rostow thesis is the idea of the 'leading sector'. The spectacular growth of the cotton industry necessarily had wide repercussions in other sectors of the economy, for instance on the growth of shipping, port facilities and inland transport, on the chemical, engineering and building industries, on iron and coal production, on housing and urban amenities (such as gas lighting and food markets), and on banking, insurance and other financial institutions. Habakkuk and Deane find these ideas stimulating, but their critical commentary on Rostow concludes:

> Except in providing an important new domestic export, or by sheer force of example, . . . it is difficult to see how the cotton industry could have *led* the national economy in any meaningful sense of the word. It served a mass market and was therefore capable of growing rapidly to a considerable size; but its inter-relations with other industries were not of a kind which would automatically stimulate expansion elsewhere. Its raw material was imported and its capital–output ratio was low. The multiplier effect of investment in cotton cannot have been very great.[88]

The contention about capital–output ratios rests on estimates of capital and output which do not accurately convey the extent of the industry (see Table 10), and it is clear from the various revisions suggested that the ratio could be much higher. It is not possible to *measure* the impact of cotton on other sectors of the economy; but the direct connection between the growth of cotton and other branches of the textile industry is well documented and easy to illustrate.

Arkwright's techniques were not difficult to apply to worsted spinning, and worsted mills modelled on his cotton mills were

[88] Habakkuk and Deane, in Rostow (ed.), *The Economics of Take-off*, p. 72.

TABLE 10

CONTRASTING ESTIMATES OF CAPITAL–OUTPUT RATIOS IN THE COTTON INDUSTRY, 1787–1803

Years	Fixed capital (£m.)	Value added (£m.)	Ratio
(1) 1787–9	2·0	4·7	1:2·3
1801–3	9·25	11·0	1:1·2
(2) 1797	2·5	16·9	1:6·8

Sources: (1) Deane and Cole, op. cit., pp. 185, 262.
(2) Table 3 (p. 30) for capital; see text for 'value added'.

soon being built in the hosiery districts of the Midlands, and in parts of Lancashire, the West Riding and Devon.[89] Cotton displaced some fabrics formerly made in worsted, but the overall effect was to stimulate it, particularly for new lines such as carpets.[90] In the linen industry, John Marshall of Leeds inaugurated the factory system by adopting Arkwright's techniques and factory organisation.[91] Wool was unsuitable for roller spinning, but easily succumbed to the mule.[92] The hosiery and lace industries were still organised under a species of the domestic system, but benefited from cheaper and finer yarns. When the power loom won acceptance in cotton, it was soon being modified for wool, worsted, linen and silk yarns. If the cotton industry did not lead the national economy, it certainly led the British and (until the early 1830s) the European and American textile industry in its technology, in the development of the factory system, and in standardised production for the popular market.

It is also possible to demonstrate some direct connections between the cotton industry and the birth of new activities in other

[89] E. M. Sigworth, *Black Dyke Mills* (Liverpool, 1958) pp. 3–6; Chapman, *The Early Factory Masters*, chap. 6.
[90] Rees, *Cyclopaedia*, article on 'Worsted Manufacture' (*c.* 1818).
[91] W. G. Rimmer, *Marshalls of Leeds, Flax Spinners* (1960).
[92] Crump and Ghorbal, *Huddersfield Woollen Industry*, pp. 60, 66.

sectors of the economy. The first multi-storey cotton mills built in the 1790s introduced the idea of iron-framed buildings, a technical innovation with far-reaching consequences for architecture and the building industry.[93] Early in the next decade these mills were among the first public buildings to be lit by gas, and the excitement with which contemporaries gazed at the illuminated mills guaranteed the spread of the technique.[94] The early factory colonies introduced new standards of working-class housing which were widely copied in the surrounding areas and helped to effect a general improvement of housing standards in the Midlands and North of England.[95] The pioneers of factory production, Arkwright, Strutt, Peel and others, had to build most of their own plant, and in so doing established the practice of using specialised machinery for mass production of components such as spindles, rollers, gear wheels and bolts.[96] The idea of *standardised* production of cotton machinery was introduced in the 1830s by Richard Roberts, the Manchester inventor of the automatic mule, and was quickly carried over into other branches of engineering, such as the building of railway locomotives.[97] The earliest railway line built for regular passenger and goods services linked Liverpool and Manchester, and the first major phase of railway construction in the 1840s Lancashire investors contributed most of the capital.[98] Many of the ironfounding, engineering and chemical firms in Lancashire, the Glasgow region, the West Riding and the Vale of Trent (Nottingham region) owed their birth or growth to the enormous stimulus given to the regional economies during Rostow's 'take-off'

[93] T. Bannister, 'The First Iron-Framed Buildings', *Architectural Review*, cvii (1950) pp. 231–46.

[94] Tann, *The Development of the Factory*, chap. 8.

[95] J. D. Chambers, *Vale of Trent* (1959) p. 62; S. D. Chapman (ed.) *The History of Working Class Housing: A Symposium* (1971).

[96] Rees, *Cyclopaedia*, article on 'Cotton'.

[97] Musson and Robinson, *Science and Technology in the Industrial Revolution*, p. 478.

[98] S. Broadbridge, 'The Early Capital Market: The Lancs. and Yorkshire Railway', *Economic History Review*, 2nd ser., viii (1955–6).

period.[99] These connections between cotton and other developments in the economy are clearly very important, but their development took place after the 'take-off period, and they are not the same as the direct multiplier effect involved in the argument of Deane and Cole. However, they could reasonably be included in Rostow's definition of the 'forward effects' of the growth of the leading sector, a dimension that is practically impossible to measure.

The controversy that followed the publication of the Rostow thesis focused particular attention on the period between 1780 and 1800. One of the merits of Deane and Cole's work is that it identifies other periods of expansion, and draws attention to the 'peak period of growth' in cotton in the quarter-century after 1815, when raw cotton imports multiplied four and a half times. Data from Ellison, a well-informed nineteenth-century writer, have been reproduced by Deane and Cole to indicate that payments to labour (wages, salaries, etc.) took a falling percentage of the gross receipts of the cotton industry in the 1820s, 1830s and 1840s, and consequently they advance the suggestion that the spectacular growth of the quarter-century was financed by 'a marked increase in the share of profit in net output' (op. cit., p. 189). The point, if it can be substantiated, has important implications for the hotly debated issue of the standard of living, as well as for investment trends. However, recent business histories offer no support for this thesis. They show that Ashworth Brothers, M'Connel & Kennedy, and Kirkman Finlay, respectively leading cotton firms in Bolton, Manchester and Glasgow, were all experiencing falling profit margins in these decades. Lee concludes his study of M'Connel & Kennedy with the view that 'productivity did not increase quick enough in this period to offset the declining [raw] cotton/yarn price margin's effects'.[100] Of course, it might be argued that these three

[99] See, e.g., Musson and Robinson, *Science and Technology in the Industrial Revolution*, chap. 13; Chapman, *The Early Factory Masters*, pp. 147–53; Hume and Butt, 'Muirkirk, 1788–1802'.

[100] Lee, *A Cotton Enterprise*, pp. 138–43; Boyson, *The Ashworth Cotton Enterprise*, pp. 27–33.

big firms were not representative of the whole industry. In the first half of the nineteenth century the average capacity of cotton mills increased thirteen times (see Table 11) as the numerous small entrepreneurs struggled to assimilate the

TABLE 11

NUMBER AND AVERAGE SIZE OF COTTON MILLS IN BRITAIN, 1797–1850

	No. of spinning factories	Approx. annual U.K. import of cotton (million lb.)	Average annual input per factory (lb.)
1797	c. 900	30	33,000
1833–4	c. 1,125	300	270,000
1850	1,407	600	430,000

Sources: Table 3 (p. 30), and E. Baines, *History of the Cotton Manufacture* (1835) p. 394; B. R. Mitchell and P. Deane, *Abstract of British Historical Statistics* (1962) pp. 178–9.

achievements of the pioneers of factory production, and it seems reasonable to suppose that rapid strides in efficiency were accompanied by thin but improving profit margins. However, we must wait for some more business histories before this problem can be decided.

Turning from investment and production (the supply side) to domestic and overseas markets (the demand side), it is necessary first of all to emphasise that British superiority in quality production had secured a firm foothold in consumer tastes before the era of the great inventors. Until recently, the superiority of eighteenth-century French copperplate cotton prints was taken for granted, but the discovery of English pattern books with a wide variety of floral and pictorial designs of high quality has convinced art historians that London and Dublin, rather than Paris, perfected the techniques of designing, engraving and colouring of printed textiles in the third quarter of the eighteenth century. The history of the ceramic and fine metal industries in the English provinces is dominated by the names of Wedgwood and

Boulton, entrepreneurs whose reputation and commercial success were based on the exploitation of a large variety of tastefully designed goods.[101] Is it too much to expect that a similar combination of design consciousness and commercial flair laid the foundation of Lancashire's great achievement? Few would doubt the plausibility of this suggestion, and the only reason it has escaped notice until recently is the historical accident that good Wedgwood and Boulton archives have survived while there has been only scattered evidence to illustrate the scale of originality of the work of the calico printers.

Defoe complained in 1725 that 'it is a hard matter to know the mistress from the maid by dress', and his remark was echoed through the remaining years of the century. In 1783 an article in the *London Magazine* lamented that 'Every servant girl has her cotton gown and her cotton stockings whilst . . . articles of wool lie mildewed in our mercers' shops', and went on to include 'others in inferior stations' with those being castigated.[102] The introduction of the Arkwright system of continuous production enormously increased the productivity of labour, and the high elasticity of demand brought a growing volume of finer cotton yarns on to the market at falling prices. T. S. Ashton collected statistical data to illustrate the trend of falling prices of fine yarns from 1795 to 1850 and of cotton cloth from 1812 to 1850. He compared the two series with one for average wages of cotton-mill operatives, and concluded that the 'fall in the cost of producing yarn and cloth was not the result of any marked fall in the price of labour'.[103] In the same period, the price of foodstuffs showed only a slight decline, and it seems reasonable to surmise that after the French Wars cotton prices led a fall in the price of textiles, and so contributed to the working-class standard of living.

[101] Cf. N. McKendrick, 'An Eighteenth Century Entrepreneur in Salesmanship and Marketing Techniques', *Economic History Review*, 2nd ser., XII (1960).

[102] Anne Buck, 'Variations in English Women's Dress in the Eighteenth Century', *Folk Life*, XI (1971) pp. 20, 24.

[103] T. S. Ashton, 'Some Statistics of the Industrial Revolution', in E. M. Carus-Wilson (ed.), *Essays in Economic History*, vol. II (1962).

If there is any substance in the contention that the Industrial Revolution period witnessed a significant rise in working-class living standards, cheaper clothing must have made a major contribution to this favourable movement for large classes of the population.

Select Bibliography

THE following short list of books and articles is intended as a guide to further reading, and not as an exhaustive bibliography. It does not include parish histories, contemporary works, unpublished theses and parliamentary papers, but some of the more important items in these categories are mentioned in the footnotes to the text, where they have been used to help fill the gaps between more important work.

The place of publication is London unless otherwise stated.

M. Blaug, 'The Productivity of Capital in the Lancashire Cotton Industry during the Nineteenth Century', *Economic History Review*, 2nd ser., xiii (1961). Assembles and analyses data for the period 1833 to 1886.

R. Boyson, *The Ashworth Cotton Enterprise* (Oxford, 1970). A valuable study of one of the best known of the second-generation firms.

John Butt (ed.), *Robert Owen, Prince of Cotton Spinners* (Newton Abbot, 1971). Chap. 7, 'Robert Owen as a Businessman', is the best account of Owen as an entrepreneur, but Owen's *Life of Robert Owen* (1857) should be read first.

D. Bythell, *The Handloom Weavers* (Cambridge, 1969). Should be read in conjunction with E. P. Thompson, *The Making of the English Working Class* (1963), as explained in Section (5).

W. H. Chaloner, *People and Industries* (1963). Contains short introductory essays on the Lombes and the Derby silk mill, Crompton, and the Cartwright brothers.

S. D. Chapman, *The Early Factory Masters* (Newton Abbot, 1967). An analysis of the origins of enterprise and problems faced by cotton-mill owners in the Midlands.

——, 'Fixed Capital Formation in the British Cotton Industry, 1770–1815', *Economic History Review*, 2nd ser., xxiii (1970). Discusses the problems and illustrates techniques for calculating capital formation during the period (see Section 4). An extended version of this article is in J. P. P. Higgins and S. Pollard (eds.), *Aspects of Capital Investment in Great Britain, 1750–1850* (1971).

——, 'The Peels in the Early English Cotton Industry', *Business History*, xi (1969). The only study of this leading firm.

Frances Collier, *The Family Economy of the Working Classes in the Cotton Industry* (Manchester, 1965). Contains material of general interest as well as analysing family income of employees in the early cotton industry.

M. M. Edwards, *The British Cotton Trade, 1780–1815* (Manchester, 1967). Closely examines the commercial development of the industry during the period, and is easily the best modern work on this aspect of the subject.

R. S. Fitton and A. P. Wadsworth, *The Strutts and the Arkwrights* (Manchester, 1958). An outstanding business history.

E. R. R. Green, *The Lagan Valley, 1800–1850* (1949). Chap. 4 covers the cotton industry in Northern Ireland.

R. L. Hills, *Power in the Industrial Revolution* (Manchester, 1970). Despite its title, this is a good layman's account of the development of textile technology. There are four chapters on the application of mechanical power.

C. H. Lee, *A Cotton Enterprise, 1795–1840: A History of M'Connel & Kennedy, Fine Cotton Spinners* (Manchester, 1972). Summarises the valuable records of this important Manchester firm.

G. M. Mitchell, 'The English and Scottish Cotton Industries', *Scottish Historical Review*, XXII (1925). Still the best single account of the Scottish industry.

F. M. Montgomery, *Printed Textiles: English and American Cottons and Linens, 1700–1850* (1970). A concise and well-illustrated account of recent research by art historians. Includes an excellent bibliography.

A. E. Musson and E. Robinson, *Science and Technology in the Industrial Revolution* (Manchester, 1969). Includes useful essays on the Lancashire chemical and engineering industries, showing how they grew out of the cotton industry.

L. S. Pressnell, *Country Banking in the Industrial Revolution* (Oxford, 1956). The standard work on the subject, illustrating the connections between cotton and banking.

A. Slaven,' A Glasgow Firm in the Indian Market: John Lean & Sons, Muslin Weavers', *Business History Review*, XLIII (1969). A good article in an area in which at present there are very few case studies.

Roland Smith, 'Manchester as a Centre for Manufacturing and Merchanting Cotton Goods, 1820–30', *University of Birmingham Historical Journal*, IV (1953–4). At present the only modern study in this area, and should be supplemented (see Section 4).

Jennifer Tann, *The Development of the Factory* (1970). Covers economic as well as technical aspects of factory building.

A. J. Taylor, 'Concentration and Specialisation in the Lancashire Cotton Industry, 1825–1850', *Economic History Review*, 2nd ser., I (1948–9). Now needs to be supplemented with H. B. Rodgers, 'The Lancashire Cotton Industry in 1840', *Transactions of the Institute of British Geographers*, XXVIII (1960), and S. D. Chapman, 'The Cost of Power in the Industrial Revolution', *Midland History*, I (1970).

G. Unwin *et al.*, *Samuel Oldknow and the Arkwrights* (Manchester, 1924). A pioneer business history that is still valuable.

A. P. Wadsworth and Julia de L. Mann, *The Cotton Trade and Industrial Lancashire, 1600–1780* (Manchester, 1931). Remains the standard work on the early period.

Index